Value TRAI®

Based Risk Management

Basic Tools For Managing
Business Threats & Opportunities

Chris Duggleby

A BizChangers Media Book

Copyright © Chris Duggleby 2011

FIRST EDITION

British Library Cataloguing in Publication Data.
A catalogue record for this book is available from the British Library.

ISBN: 978 09566 7770 9

Bizchangers Ltd.
9 Ashton Court, Victoria Way
Woking GU21 6AL
England

For information Chris Duggleby can be contacted by the e-mail link at
www.ChrisDuggleby.com.

Chris Duggleby is the proprietor of the Registered Trade Marks listed below. The use of these Registered Trade Marks for commercial gain requires prior written permission from the Registered Trade Mark proprietor.

Registered Trade Marks:

- value TRAI
- DOSER workshop
- V&LI
- V&LIUMM
- ExposureTracker
- strategy SWEAT
- t-TRAI
- trans4map
- plan4mation
- bizchangers

This book is dedicated to
Christine Helen Duggleby
in recognition of 70 years of
dedicated service to others.

Contents

Chris Duggleby

I. Introduction

The value of a business enterprise depends on its ability to manage risk. For a business to be profitable and grow it must take on risks and manage them better than its competitors. These risks can be either opportunities or threats. Threats are defined as risks which have the potential to negatively influence business value; whereas opportunities create positive value potential.

Sometimes threats and opportunities simply reflect two different ways of viewing a single situation. For example, one way to create a successful business is to take something generally considered to be a threat and, by managing its negative impact, turn it into an opportunity. Burglar alarm and fire extinguisher manufacturers use this approach. They take the threat of a burglary or fire and turn it into a profitable business opportunity.

In addition to producing opportunities out of threats it is also possible to create threats by mismanaging opportunities. A typical example of this situation is found when major construction projects are late or over budget due to poor project management capability. Mismanagement can turn an idea, initially considered to be an excellent opportunity, into an economic disaster.

To address the close interaction which can exist between threats and opportunities business risk management needs to consider both.

The ability of a business to manage risks does not just influence its profitability; it can also impact its cost of borrowing. Financial institutions evaluate businesses from a risk perspective when deciding which premium to charge when lending money. Companies with a low risk credit rating can expect to pay a lower lending premium compared to others perceived to be a higher credit risk. Banks charge more for loans to higher risk companies to compensate for the greater probability that the business will not be able to promptly repay its obligations to them.

Investors in the stock market have traditionally evaluated companies using two criteria. They look at the level of risk associated with the markets being pursued by the company and also make an assessment of the company's ability to manage that risk. Shareholders expect bigger returns from higher risk businesses and will therefore expect bigger dividends or a faster increase in the value of the company's share price to justify their investment. Generally this means they will pay less for the shares of a company with a poor track record in risk management.

The ability of a company to manage risk also affects its cost of recruiting good employees. Employees desire long term security for their jobs and pensions as well as a good level of remuneration for their work and experience. Companies perceived as having a higher level of risk will have to pay more to find and keep capable staff. Employees who are prepared to compromise on job security and sell themselves to a high risk, high paying employer will be more likely to sell themselves to another employer as soon as a better offer appears.

This does not mean that risk is bad. In fact risky ventures are essential for our continued prosperity and security. The value that can be created from turning threats into business opportunities has already been mentioned. Today the reduced availability of natural resources increasingly forces us to look at high risk locations and apply newer, sometimes untried, technology in order to find and transport the remaining oil, gas and mineral deposits. Companies also need to enter into new kinds of business relationships and joint ventures to reduce their risk exposure and open the door to these new opportunities. If businesses do not take on these risks they will not be able to supply the energy and other raw materials which are essential to our modern existence.

Therefore a key factor for our future prosperity will be the effective application of business risk management processes. Two companies may go after the same profitable business opportunity but if one is able to manage the risks better this will help it to derive more, longer term, value from the business. With time the benefits of lower cost products and logistics will be passed onto consumers. A company with a consistent track record for efficiently and effectively managing risks will find its cost of borrowing and employing capable people is lower compared with its higher risk competitors. If a company's business has the potential to put people's safety or the environment at risk an effective risk management programme will lead to higher employee motivation, a better image among customers and a good reputation with authorities making them more willing to grant operating permits.

The purpose of this book is to introduce business people to efficient, effective risk management processes. It describes simple tools which will help a company to embed a risk management culture and philosophy throughout its organisation. The primary focus of these tools and processes is to minimise the potential value loss from threats and maximise the potential value gained from opportunities.

The book introduces the concept of a **Risk Subject**. This can be any part of a business organisation, large or small, which is used as the initial subject in a risk identification and evaluation process. A risk subject can be an individual's job, a business entity (e.g. a company, division, department or office), a project, or a process. The risk management tools and processes introduced here can be applied to any risk subject.

A risk is defined as important using the concept of 'risk subject materiality'. Material risks are those with the potential to significantly influence the value of the risk subject from which they have been identified. This ensures that the people in the risk subject who will be involved with identifying and evaluating risks appreciate the relevance of what they are doing. This is an important factor in encouraging local participation and understanding. Therefore a stores person is just as motivated to identify risks in the storeroom as a Chief Financial Officer identifying risks to the company balance sheet.

Risk importance is based on two criteria; the likelihood of risk occurrence and the influence a risk has on business value when it occurs. The risk management processes described here will pay special attention to understanding and managing these two areas; likelihood of occurrence and influence on value. Systems will be introduced to monitor and track the activities required to manage important risks.

To be effective risk management needs to be embedded into the culture of an organisation and become one of its core capabilities. It should not be the exclusive domain of a group of risk specialists. If they exist, risk specialists should be the enablers of the risk management process. They do this by supporting the design and improvement of risk management systems, providing risk management training and by facilitating risk workshops. They are not the implementers of the system; everybody is!

Companies which have embedded risk management in their corporate culture thrive in periods of change because they are better equipped than their competitors to derive value from uncertainty. These companies evolve quickly when the business environment undergoes rapid and unpredictable change. If we consider Darwin's evolutionary principle of 'Survival of the fittest', the risk management companies are the business 'survivors'. They will be the fittest when it comes to harnessing value from their changing environment; they compete better for scarce resources; their activities and structures are cost focused but they are also highly adaptable and responsive to change and the opportunities it can bring.

Value creation is how success in managing threats and opportunities is measured. All the tools described here are focussed on the value which can be derived from, or protected by, managing risks. To protect shareholder value, risk management has become an essential component of modern corporate governance. Around the World regulatory bodies require that companies and their auditors monitor the use of effective risk management systems to provide assurance that risks to investor's funds are being appropriately addressed. The oversight of these systems is a key role for non-executive directors of public companies.

This book explains how to design and implement business risk management systems. It builds upon the author's 30 years' experience of managing chemical businesses around the globe. In the chemicals business poor management of risks can kill people or lead to environmental disasters. Therefore, effective risk management should be a leader's first priority. In many places the book refers to business value when considering how to evaluate risk. The value destroyed by threats which influence people's health, their livelihoods or the environment should not be underestimated. If a single life is at threat try to consider what it would be worth to you to avoid losing the person you love most. If a threat has environmental consequences, try to imagine the full cost to your own life and community if the event occurred in your back yard.

The tools described in the following chapters will help businesses to benefit from the authors personal experience. The ability of the chemicals industry to effectively manage risks has helped some companies generate respectable profits for their shareholders. However, when the controls to manage these risks break down, the economic and personal losses can be astronomical. This book draws upon first-hand experiences of failures as well as successes.

The tools can be applied as part of a corporate-wide risk management system or they can be tried out first in an individual business unit, project or process. If a business needs to transform urgently, the simplicity of this approach will facilitate quick implementation. Special chapters focus on the management of risks during transformation projects.

A four part classification system is used to describe the categories of value elements which are applicable to any risk subject. This ensures a simple, consistent framework and standardised vocabulary. This unified language enables the same tools to be applied in all business entities, projects, processes and in every job. The book starts by introducing this classification system and goes on to explain the core risk management tools.

In later chapters more attention will be given to the design of company-wide risk exposure tracking and control systems and the implementation of risk management techniques to business transformation projects.

Most businesses in urgent need of restructuring will find themselves resource constrained. In the past many corporations have turned to consultancies to help them implement risk management systems. This can be expensive and the commitment from third parties can sometimes be transient, with only qualified accountability for delivery. A more fundamental solution is to try and embed the appropriate skills, knowledge and systems within the transforming organisation. This is an approach which is promoted here, with the focus on self help and cost efficiency.

II. Risk Subjects and Value TRAIs

Before starting a risk evaluation process it is necessary to understand and clearly define what is being evaluated. This 'what' is referred to as the **Risk Subject**. It can be almost any part of a business; a job, a project, a process, or an entity like a division, department, or even the company itself.

The Risk Subject

A risk subject can undergo a risk evaluation as a stand-alone unit regardless of its size or complexity. The basic approach to identifying, evaluating and acting upon risks is the same, regardless of the risk subject's purpose or its context. Before carrying out these risk management activities the risk subject's composition and its business purpose must be defined.

If the area undergoing risk evaluation is very large or highly complex it may be appropriate to break it down into smaller, more manageable units. This makes it easier to investigate the risks involved in greater detail. For example, at the company level risk evaluation tends to concentrate on big strategic risks which have the potential to influence the company's share price and the dividends it can pay to shareholders. At the other end of the scale, by evaluating risks to an individual person's job or the basic processes they perform; threats or opportunities may be uncovered which are overlooked at the company level. For example, an employee may be in a unique position to identify an innovative new product opportunity or a major threat to the safety of his or her colleagues. Both of these items may not be known to the board of directors of the company but they may have the potential to impact the company's strategy, performance or its share price.

Some typical approaches for breaking down larger risk areas into smaller more manageable risk subjects are described below:

- **Entity** based split: a company (the largest entity) can be subdivided into divisions (smaller entities) which, if required, can be further subdivided into departments. Any of these entities can be considered as a risk subject.

- **Process** based split: an entity can be subdivided based on its major processes which, if required, can be further subdivided using smaller sub-processes. Any of these processes or sub-processes can be considered as a risk subject.

- **Job** based split: a Company or entity can be subdivided based on its existing hierarchy of employees. Here any job in the organisation from the Chief Executive down to the most junior employee can be considered as a risk subject.

Using these approaches, or some combination of them, it is possible to create a risk subject hierarchy. In such a hierarchy the high-level risk subjects contain, and are responsible for, a number of smaller low-level risk subjects. Risks influencing a high-level risk subject can be estimated by combining the risks identified from all of its constituent lower level risk subjects.

For example, consider a team comprising a manager and six employees reporting to that manager. If each employee is evaluated as a risk subject the risks from all 6 employees can be combined to become part of the manager's risk profile. Each employee is accountable for his or her activities and the risks associated with them. The manager is, in turn, accountable for the activities and the associated risks of all six employees as well as his or her own activities and risks.

The actual selection of the most suitable hierarchical framework for risk subjects is governed by the nature of the business, the existing organisational structure and the level of detail or 'granularity' required from the risk evaluation process. For example, a manufacturing operation using a number of different production processes may be more suited to a process based organisation of risk subjects. Alternatively a conglomerate of discrete business units or companies may be more suited to an entity based approach.

Wherever possible it is recommended to try and use the existing organisational structure as a basis for defining risk subject hierarchies. This will eliminate the need for separate risk management structures and help to minimise cost and complexity. Therefore the starting point for defining a hierarchy of risk subjects is normally the company's organisation chart. This works best in an organisation in which everyone has clear accountability for the activities of the people below them. Here, the risk subjects can be identical to people's jobs. This approach ensures all entities in the organisation, like departments, are included because they will each be the responsibility (or job) of a specific manager. Special projects and important processes in the company will also have managers, so a purely job based approach will also include the evaluation of risks to projects and processes.

Another advantage of using the organisation chart as the basic framework for risk evaluation is that it is usually the quickest approach to get off the ground.

Risk Subject Materiality

A key output from risk evaluation is the ranking of risks based on their relative importance to the business. Only those risks considered to be important are subjected to a detailed evaluation. This helps to ensure risk management is focused and efficient. The importance of each risk is measured by its potential to influence the value of the business. Risks with a significant influence on business value are described as 'material'.

Materiality is determined in relation to the potential influence of a risk on the value of the risk subject for which it has been identified. Therefore a risk's materiality will depend on the size and scope of the risk subject. Although it can vary from business to business, a risk can be defined as material if it has the potential to influence 5% or more of the annual value created, invested or protected by the risk subject.

When the risk subject is a complete business, the materiality can be defined as 5% of its average annual profit. If the risk subject is a project the equivalent materiality benchmark can be 5% of the average annual investment in that project. In some cases the main purpose of a risk subject is to protect value. This is the case for a risk subject which is a fire fighting department at a manufacturing site. Here 5% of the value of assets protected by the fire fighting department can be used as the benchmark when deciding whether a risk is material.

Using this approach, risks identified as material for a higher level risk subject (e.g. a company) must have a bigger influence on value in order to be defined as material compared with risks identified for lower level risk subjects (e.g. a department or a small project). As already explained important risks can get overlooked if only company level materiality is used during the initial risk identification process. In large organisations the use of a risk subject hierarchy can ensure more focussed identification of risks at lower levels. This focus arises because materiality is defined in relation to the risk subject where the risk is first identified. This is the concept of **Risk Subject Materiality**. In addition to providing focus it also helps to ensure that people within the risk subject feel ownership and appreciate the relevance of the risks they are identifying.

To illustrate this, consider the job of a maintenance engineer which has been defined as a risk subject. This job is at a relatively junior level in the company's hierarchy. The engineer may identify the inconsistent availability of spares for a key machine to be a material risk to his or her job. The person has detailed knowledge of equipment maintenance issues which more senior managers in the company do not have. At the company level this risk may not even be identified, and even if it is, its materiality may not be appreciated. However, the specific risk identified by the engineer may have the potential to cause a major production breakdown and have a profound impact on the value of the company. In such circumstances a bottom-up approach to risk management is more likely to identify such risks and with the right risk management process they can then be escalated to receive the appropriate level of attention.

Targets and TAPs

Although any part of a business can be evaluated as a risk subject there are two essential requirements which every risk subject needs. First of all the risk subject must have a clear set of **Targets**. These are used to measure success in delivering, investing or protecting value. Here value is not just short term financial performance (e.g. profitability) but also takes into account longer term strategic value to the business (e.g. balance sheet value; business good will; employee motivation; health, safety and environmental issues).

The second essential requirement for every risk subject is a person who is accountable for delivering the targets. This person is referred to as the Target Accountable Person or **TAP**. If the risk subject is an entity like a division or a department the TAP is the manager of that division or department. If the risk subject is an individual job the TAP is the person who does that job. For projects and processes the TAP is the leader in charge of the project or process. For each risk subject the TAP, in addition to being accountable for the delivery of business targets, is also responsible for the management of any risks which could influence the delivery of those targets. This linkage is essential to ensure that everyone in a leadership position identifies risk management as an integral part of their accountability for delivering business targets.

Value Elements and the Value TRAI

In order to identify risks to business value each risk subject must be broken down into its main value components. Risks are identified, ranked and evaluated based on their potential to influence business value. These risks (both opportunities and threats) can influence value in a number of ways. To ensure important risks are not overlooked an approach is used which takes into account the range and diversity of ways in which value can be influenced. This range and diversity is addressed by identifying a set of key **Value Elements** for the risk subject. Each value element is an important contributor to the delivery of business value. A risk which influences a value element is therefore also likely to have an impact on the creation or protection of business value. This is why a carefully constructed set of value elements are an important component in the risk identification process.

Value elements are divided into four categories using the **value TRAI** classification. The word TRAI (pronounced 'tray') is an abbreviation based on the names of four categories of value elements, any one of which could potentially be influenced by a threat or opportunity. These are Targets, Resources, Activities and Interactions.

Within each of these main categories a more detailed set of value elements defines the purpose and composition of the risk subject. These are used in the risk identification process.

Value TRAI	
T…	TARGETS
R…	RESOURCES
A…	ACTIVITIES
I…	INTERACTIONS

T	Targets	Profit; Safety
R	Resources	People; Raw Materials; Energy; Machines
A	Activities	Production; Sales; Administration
I	Interactions	with Customers; Authorities; Banks

Table 1: Examples of Value Elements

In the value TRAI the targets measure whether the risk subject has delivered or protected business value. They can include the targets the company already uses to evaluate the risk subject's performance. As well as measuring performance in delivering value these targets are used to assess the influence risks have on that delivery. The targets should reflect both short and long term value creation by the business. The exact selection of targets for a particular risk subject will depend on whether the subject is evaluated on its own or as part of a hierarchy.

Targets can be specific or generic. **Specific Value Targets** are unique to an individual risk subject. They can be described as 'bespoke' and are particularly relevant if the risk subject creates value for the business in a unique way, for example, if the risk subject involves a unique process or product. **Generic Value Targets** are used when there is an intention to collate information from several risk subjects about risks which influence more general targets. For example, "Safe Operations" could be a generic target which is used throughout a company.

Often a combination of generic and specific value targets is appropriate. This ensures that business targets considered to be strategic are used throughout the organisation but at the same time allows for local customisation. Customisation allows the TAP to identify specific targets which are relevant to his or her risk subject's unique situation but are not necessarily applicable to the rest of the organisation. For example, a sales department may consider 'customer satisfaction' to be an important value target whereas the site security department may find this target meaningless.

When generic targets are used throughout a company it is possible to produce a corporate risk exposure profile for each generic target. This requires a standardised approach to gathering and documenting risk exposures from several risk subjects. Later, the ExposureTracker will be introduced which supports this standardised approach. This is a simple risk database system which has the potential to collate risk information from across the company.

The other three categories in the value TRAI classification are:

- **Resources**: required by the risk subject in order to operate
- **Activities**: performed by the risk subject
- **Interactions**: with other parties, which the risk subject needs in order to deliver its targets

All the contributors to value creation or protection fall into one of these three categories. Key contributors are referred to as the value elements. The value targets, mentioned above, are used to assess the importance of each contributor to the delivery of business value. All significant business risks express themselves by influencing the delivery of value targets via resources, activities or interactions.

For example, any business entity, process or job will require a number of key resources (**R**). These may be raw materials, energy or utilities. In this context resources may also be machines, people or support systems like computer hard- and software.

Every business area must perform certain activities (**A**). For example if the risk subject is a sales department its key activities will include sales visits and customer order administration. If the risk subject is a construction project its key activities will include planning, design, procurement and implementation.

Every business area will also need to interact (**I**) with the people and organisations in its business environment. The key interactions of a sales department may be with; customers, the production planning office, and the logistics department. If the risk subject is a whole company, typical important interactions will be with shareholders, authorities and the providers of corporate finance.

The simple diagram on the following page illustrates the relationship between an enterprise's existing organisational hierarchy, some typical risk subjects and their value TRAIs.

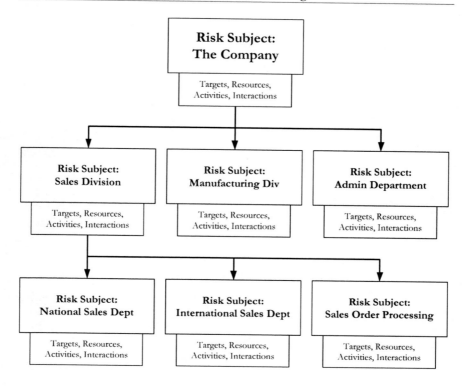

Figure 1: Typical Organisational Hierarchy, Risk Subjects and their Value TRAIs

Summary

*Prior to evaluation of risks it is necessary to describe the enterprise in terms of **risk subjects**. These can be the same as the units used in the existing organisational framework (e.g. entities or jobs). They can also represent unique or specialised areas like projects or processes. Risk evaluation can then focus on each specific area within the organisation, for example, a single department, project or process. If this area is not too complex it may be possible to evaluate its risks as a single risk subject. Alternatively it may be necessary to subdivide a more complex risk subject into several simpler (or lower level) ones to provide the required level of risk detail. This is described as a **risk subject hierarchy**. The **value TRAI** classification is used to create a profile of how each risk subject creates or protects value. This profile is made up of key **value elements**. An advantage of the risk subject/value TRAI approach is that it is versatile, flexible and allows risk information from several risk subjects to be collated and consolidated. It can be used to identify risks which influence any business situation and provide the required level of detail.*

Chris Duggleby

The value TRAI categories and their value elements will now be described in more detail.

Targets

Every risk subject has a business purpose. Success in achieving this purpose is measured against targets and when everything goes according to plan the risk subject delivers these targets in full and on time. Risks, both threats and opportunities, have the potential to influence the successful delivery of the targets. Targets therefore provide an important benchmark against which we can assess and compare how risks influence business value.

Once a risk subject has been selected, its main business purpose or purposes, together with an appropriate set of key targets are identified. Targets may already be included in a performance plan or budget if the risk subject is an established business entity. In this case the existing targets can be reviewed to determine if they are suitable benchmarks for assessing the influence of risks on the value of the business. These can then be included in the key targets for the risk subject.

Business value must be considered from both a short and a long term perspective. An example of a short term value target is the profit the business is expected to make in the current accounting period. Longer term value is usually reflected by changes in a company's balance sheet and its ability to generate future profits.

Targets relating to reputation or good ethical practice tend to have a longer term influence on the value of a business. They may, for example, increase customer and stakeholder goodwill or the value of the company's brands. Such items improve the potential for future profits by making it easier for an enterprise to get operating permits, grants or subsidies from authorities. The long term value of reputational targets should therefore not be underestimated.

If the company is listed on a stock exchange, any changes in its business value, that the public is aware of, will be reflected in its share price. For most listed companies the share price is a simple indicator of how the value of the enterprise is perceived by the market. For such companies the share price can be used as a corporate level target which measures the perceived ability of the business to deliver shareholder value.

For each risk subject one person is identified as the Target Accountable Person or 'TAP'. This person agrees the targets with more senior management and then is responsible for delivering them. Ideally the TAP is the current manager or leader of this business area. The advantage of using the existing manager as the TAP is that he or she will be familiar with many of the risks to performance delivery. The TAP plays an important role in selecting appropriate targets which will measure the influence important risks have on the value of the business. When one person is accountable

TAP

TARGET
ACCOUNTABLE
PERSON

for both business delivery and risk management the need for a separate risk management organisation is eliminated. This helps to embed risk management awareness and ownership in the existing organisation.

The TAP is also responsible for monitoring that risk management actions are being completed and sets up regular risk reviews for the risk subject. Risk management is not a 'one-off' process but must be considered as an ongoing part of normal business activities.

Each target needs a clear relationship with business value because the targets are used as the basis for assessing the relative importance of risks. Risk importance is a combination of the influence a risk has on business value and the likelihood of this level of influence happening. If the relationship between a value TRAI target and value is clear this makes the evaluation of risks which influence delivery of that target more straightforward.

For example, consider a component manufacturing business in which the target for component production is 'to make a $1m contribution to profit per month'. A strike among employees is identified as a risk to achieving this target. The influence of the strike will be to reduce manufacturing output by up-to 50%. Therefore the potential influence on business value of this risk is a loss of contribution to profit of $0.5m for each month that the strike continues. The clear relationship between the production target and business value makes it easier to assess the influence the strike will have on business value.

Typical Targets for a Risk Subject

Here are examples of some typical business targets which can be used when defining the T category in a risk subject's Value TRAI:

- **Financial Targets** (cash, profit, cost, share price)
- **Sales Targets** (revenue, turnover, gross/net contribution)
- **Production/Service Targets** (quantity, quality, rate)
- **Procurement Targets** (efficiency, expenditure)
- **Capital or Revenue Targets** (expenditure, investment)
- **Economic Targets** (return on investment, average capital employed)
- **Employee Targets** (salaries, headcount, behaviours, motivation)
- **Opinion Rating Targets** (customers, suppliers, public, employees)
- **Technology or Intellectual Targets** (Patents, Brands, Trade Marks)
- **Health, Safety, Security, Environmental Targets**
- **Aspirational Targets** (ethics, reputation, competitive rankings)

If the risk subject is relatively simple (e.g. a small department or process) it may only require a few key targets. For example a small sales department may only need four targets; sales revenue, number of customers contacted, staff turnover, and on-time payments. A simple manufacturing process might select: production volume, product quality, machine-downtime, and employee injury rate.

In addition to identifying the type of target (using a general heading for example 'profit' or 'sales revenue') a metric is also needed to quantify more specifically what successful delivery will look like. This metric tells you exactly how much of the target needs to be delivered and by when. When describing targets it is important to also specify the time frame for delivery. For example, should the target be achieved every month, every year or within 5 or 10 years?

In a hierarchy of risk subjects it is possible to use generic 'headings' for certain targets. The generic target heading is applied throughout the hierarchy together with specific metrics which are adapted to each individual risk subject. For example, if 'Sales Expansion' is the generic target heading, individual departments may be expected to expand their sales of specific products by different amounts: they will therefore each have a different sales expansion metric. In a hardware shop, for example, one department's annual target may be 'to increase sales of widgets by 5%' whereas another department may have the target 'to increase sales of tools by 10%'.

Generic targets can be an important way of cascading a company's strategic objectives down through the organisation. The risks which influence these targets at lower levels in the organisation can then be collated and combined to provide a company level assessment of the risk exposure faced by each strategic objective. Building this into a corporate risk exposure database can generate a powerful, holistic assessment of risks having the potential to influence the delivery of a company's strategy. The ExposureTracker, which will be introduced later in the book, is a risk management tool which facilitates this process.

Some typical generic target headings and metrics are provided on the table on the next pages.

Ideally the number of key targets for a risk subject should not exceed ten. If a larger number of targets are required this probably indicates that the area under evaluation needs sub-dividing using one of the risk subject hierarchy approaches described above. This will create smaller, more focused, risk subjects which require a smaller number of targets.

Target headings	Target metrics
1. Revenue	$XXX total sales value
	$XXX value/all units sold or made
2. Variable Cash Cost	$XXX total cash cost
	$XXX cash cost/all units
3. Investment Cost	$XXX total investment
	$XXX investment/unit
4. Production Rate	Total units made
	Units made/hour
5. Employee Cost	$XXX total staff cost
	$XXX staff cost/all units
6. Competitive Rank	Rank v Competitors
	Products ranked 1-3 in the market
7. Safety	Injuries/employee
	Incident rate
8. Environment	Emission rate
	Transgression rate
9. Business Growth	Profit v last year
	5 year profit trend
10. KPI Delivery*	Annual KPI achievement rate (A)
	Annual KPI achievement rate (B)

*KPI's are Key Performance Indicators
which may be used to measure the performance in a business.

Table 2: Examples of Generic Target Headings and Metrics

Resources

After identifying a risk subject's targets the next stage in preparing its value TRAI requires the identification of the key resources needed to deliver these targets. Resources can be physical, economic or knowledge based (e.g. IT systems or technology). They include both fixed resources like machinery, buildings and permanent employees and variable resources such as consumable raw materials, utilities and temporary contract staff.

The value TRAI summarises the resources which are considered important to the delivery of business value. The importance of a resource can be assessed against its potential to impact the targets described above. As a rough guide if the changed availability or function of a resource impacts 5% or more of annual value created or protected by a risk subject it is material.

Although financial value is an important factor when deciding whether a resource is important it is not necessarily the only criterion. It is quite possible that items of low face value are absolutely critical for target delivery. This may be the case, for example, with a process catalyst, a product brand name or a piece of unique technical know-how. The value of these items in the balance sheet may sometimes be modest but the business may not be able to survive without them.

It is also important not to overlook 'non-physical' resources like staff capability or business systems and processes. If in doubt, consider what would happen if the resource is suddenly, and unexpectedly, unavailable. Is it easy to replace? Will the replacement be economical? Can the replacement be made available quickly?

Typical Resources for a Risk Subject

The following are examples of some typical resource Value Elements:

- **Financial Resources** (Cash, Loans, Working Capital)
- **Real Estate Resources** (Buildings, Land)
- **Equipment Resources** (Machines, Tools, Computers)
- **Resources from Authorities** (Government Permits, Licences, Grants, Incentives)
- **Knowledge Resources** (Technology, Licenses, Experience)
- **Good Will Resources** (Reputation, Brands, Intellectual Property)
- **Utility Resources** (Water, Consumable Chemicals, Waste removal)
- **Employee Resources** (Permanent and Contractual)
- **Capability Resources** (Skills, Competencies, Experience)
- **Systems Resources** (Accounting, Payments, Invoicing, IT, HR)
- **Energy Resources** (Oil, Gas, Electricity, other sources of Fuel)
- **Raw Material Resources** (Manufacturing/Service Consumables)

The risk subject's TAP (Target Accountable Person) should agree with senior management which resources are required to deliver the value targets. Normally 15 key resource elements are sufficient to identify the important risks which are likely to significantly influence the performance of a risk subject.

Activities

The activities category in the value TRAI describes what a risk subject does in order to create or protect value. Activities use, consume or convert resources in order to deliver the targets. If the risk subject is a company the activities will be its major business activities, processes or functions. At this high level the value TRAI activities are very broad in scope. They are actually composites of all the activities carried out by lower level risk subjects. These activities may be referred to as strategic activities and they are used when carrying out a 'strategic' risk analysis. If the risk subject is a lower level entity, for example, a small department, its value TRAI activities will be much more focused and can be used for a more detailed 'operational' risk analysis.

Sometimes the activities (or processes) of high level risk subjects are used as the basis for dividing complex business areas into simpler risk subjects. For example it may not be possible to split a manufacturing division into clearly compartmentalised entities because of a large number of shared services, employees or operations. In this case the major activities or processes in the manufacturing division can be used to split it into smaller, more focused, process based risk subjects. These simpler risk subjects help to ensure risks are identified which may get overlooked in a higher level evaluation.

A typical activity or process based hierarchy for sub-dividing high level risk subjects is illustrated on the next page:

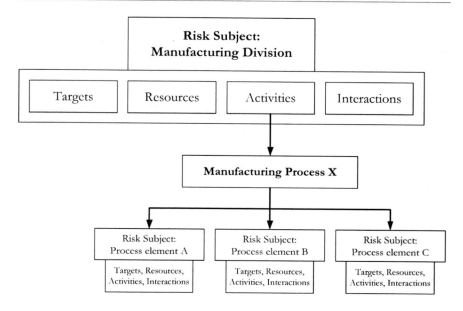

Figure 2: Typical Activity or Process based Hierarchy

In this example the information about risks identified using the value TRAIs of the process elements A, B, and C, can be combined to provide a composite risk profile for the total manufacturing process X.

This is another example of a risk subject hierarchy being used to divide a complex area into its component parts for more detailed risk analysis.

A similar approach can also be used for breaking down the activities of complex projects. Projects can usually be divided into a series of project 'life-cycle' phases. These phases represent the main activities found in most types of project. Each life-cycle phase is then used as the basis for defining a risk subject. This process is explained in more detail in chapter IX: Transformation Project Risk.

Typical Activities for a Risk Subject

The following is a list of some typical groups of activities:

- Manufacturing or Service Operations
- Selling, Marketing, Advertising, Promoting, Logistics
- Managing, Administrating, Planning, Accounting, Reporting
- Training, Supporting, Advising, Assuring
- Specialist/Technical Activities (Finance, Legal, R&D, QA, etc.)
- Developing, Researching, Designing, Inventing
- Constructing Equipment or Buildings
- Implementing Projects

In order to keep risk evaluation focused, the value TRAI for an individual risk subject should not exceed 10 key activities. If this does not provide sufficient detail the subject should be subdivided into lower level risk subjects.

Interactions

Business enterprises do not perform their activities in a vacuum. They all need to interact with the outside world. This applies at all levels within a company. Generally speaking most activities produce either products or services, which something or someone outside of the risk subject needs or desires. 'Outside' can mean something or someone outside the company or it can refer to another risk subject within the same company. In addition risk subjects must interact with suppliers in order to economically obtain resources. Risk subjects, therefore, use interactions to deliver or to receive items needed to carry out their activities and deliver their targets.

The entities with which the risk subject interacts are referred to as its **stakeholders**. Some stakeholders want the risk subject to satisfy their needs or desires for products or services. Other stakeholders satisfy the needs or desires of the risk subject. These needs or desires can be physical like goods, chemicals or energy, or they can be non-physical like information, services, or entertainment.

One way to identify interactions is to draw up a list of all the stakeholders associated with the risk subject. The relevant needs or desires emanating from either the risk subject or the stakeholder are then identified. Often the interaction is a two way process: customers need products, the producer wants their money; employees want money, the employer needs their work. Understanding such mutual relationships can be very important to the identification of risks and suitable ways to manage how they influence business value.

When a risk subject produces products or services these are included in its value TRAI as interactions. This is because the product or service actually satisfies some desire or need of the other party: it represents one component of an interaction. With products it is important not to simply think in terms of the physical items. Consider the role or need that the product fulfils for the customer. The customer usually identifies the product as a 'package' which, in addition to the physical product, includes things like quality of service and performance, reliability and speed of delivery. This holistic view of products and services as interactions helps to identify risks associated with profitably satisfying customer expectations.

Interactions also exist with outside agencies, for example, when securing permits or licences to operate. These interactions may be with Local Authorities or Government Agencies. The permit or licence was described above as a resource, but the way to obtain and keep it requires interactions with the appropriate bodies. For high level risk subjects, like companies or major projects, interactions may also be necessary with the providers of finance, politicians or the media.

After identifying the interactions rank them in terms of their importance to the risk subject – paying particular attention to how they influence the risk subject's ability to create or protect value. This process is sometimes imprecise and an element of informed subjective judgement is required. It may help to consider what would happen if the interaction does not occur. Will this influence the risk subject's ability to create or protect value? Is the financial or reputational impact large? Are their alternatives or contingences? Can they be implemented quickly? The final decision about which interactions to include is made by the TAP. Ideally the value TRAI should have no more than 15 key interaction Value Elements.

Typical Stakeholders for a Risk Subject

The following is a list of some typical stakeholders:

- Customers

- Suppliers

- Competitors

- Employees (Permanent and Temporary) and their Representatives

- Owners, Shareholders, Lenders, Auditors

- Governments (Local, Regional, National, International)

- Non-governmental Authorities, Rule Makers

- Industrial Bodies and Creators of Standards

- Interest, Pressure, and Lobby Groups

- General Public, Representatives and Influencers

- (For internal risk subjects) other Departments, Functions

When preparing value TRAIs try to avoid getting distracted by debates about whether a value element belongs in one category or another. For example, are business consultants resources or interactions? If the value element is an important component of business value for the risk subject just make sure it is included in the value TRAI somewhere. The main purpose of the value TRAI classification is help identify all the important risks. It should be used as a quick, simple tool and not slow down the risk evaluation process by becoming a bureaucratic burden.

Summary

The **Value TRAI** is a simple tool which can be applied to any risk subject. It describes the risk subject using **Value Elements**. These value elements are grouped into four categories: targets, resources, activities and interactions. For risk identification purposes the value TRAI only contains those value elements which are important to creating or protecting the value of the risk subject.

Examples

For illustration purposes some simple examples of value TRAIs are given on the following pages. The first table is an empty template: columns are included into which targets, resources, activities and interactions can be added. Following this are three examples of simple value TRAIs. These are from various parts of an imaginary company called CarNob Ltd. This company manufactures and sells small, but essential, components for the Auto industry.

Risk Subject Name: _____

Targets	Resources (see next page)	Activities (see next page)	Interactions (see next page)
1	1	1	1
2	2	2	2
3	3	3	3
4	4	4	4
5	5	5	5
6	6	6	6
7	7	7	7
8	8	8	8
9	9	9	9
10	10	10	10
	11		11
	12		12
	13		13
	14		14
	15		15
Ideally 10 max	Ideally 15 max	Ideally 10 max	Ideally 15 max

Table 3: Value TRAI template

Examples of Resources

- **Financial Resources** (Cash, Loans, Working Capital)
- **Real Estate Resources** (Buildings, Land)
- **Equipment Resources** (Machines, Tools, Computers)
- **Resources from Authorities** (Government Permits, Licences, Grants, Incentives)
- **Knowledge Resources** (Technology, Licenses, Experience)
- **Good Will Resources** (Reputation, Brands, Intellectual Property)
- **Utility Resources** (Water, Consumable Chemicals, Waste removal)
- **Employee Resources** (Permanent and Contractual)
- **Capability Resources** (Skills, Competencies, Experience)
- **Systems Resources** (Accounting, Payments, Invoicing, IT, HR)
- **Energy Resources** (Oil, Gas, Electricity, other sources of Fuel)
- **Raw Material Resources** (Manufacturing/Service Consumables)

Examples of Activities

- Manufacturing or Service Operations
- Selling, Marketing, Advertising, Promoting, Logistics
- Managing, Administrating, Planning, Accounting, Reporting
- Training, Supporting, Advising, Assuring
- Specialist/Technical Activities (Finance, Legal, R&D, QA, etc.)
- Developing, Researching, Designing, Inventing
- Constructing Equipment or Buildings
- Implementing Projects

Examples of Stakeholders for Interactions

- Customers

- Suppliers

- Competitors

- Employees (Permanent and Temporary) and their Representatives

- Owners, Shareholders, Lenders, Auditors

- Governments (Local, Regional, National, International)

- Non-governmental Authorities, Rule Makers

- Industrial Bodies and Creators of Standards

- Interest, Pressure, and Lobby Groups

- General Public, Representatives and Influencers

- (For internal risk subjects) other Departments, Functions

Examples of Value TRAIs for Simple Risk Subjects

CARNOB LTD: RISK SUBJECT 1
National Sales Department

Targets

- Sell 500,000 CarNobs this year
- Achieve an annual average CarNob price of $20 per unit
- Initiate business with 5 new customers by year end
- Reduce late payers to 10% of total transactions

Resources

- Departmental Budget $450,000/annum
- 4 Sales Representatives, 1 Sales Manager, 3 Admin Staff
- Access to company IT system with 8 terminals, 2 printers
- 8 Office phones, 5 mobile phones & running costs
- 5 leased cars and parking facilities near office
- Open plan office and utilities for 8 work stations
- Allocation (based on head count) of company systems

Activities

- Selling to domestic customers
- Visiting customers to negotiate agreements
- Receiving orders by phone
- Entry of orders into company IT system
- Ensuring timely payment by customers

Interactions

- Existing Customers
- New Customers
- Production Department
- Quality Control Manager
- Accounting Department
- Car Leasing Company
- IT Department

CarNob Ltd: Risk Subject 2
Manufacturing Process

Targets

- Manufacture 500,000 'on-spec' CarNobs this year
- Reduce CarNob off-spec rate to 5% of production by year end
- Achieve an annual average CarNob variable cost of $6 per unit
- Carry out 2 new CarNob manufacturing trials by year end
- Reduce machine down-time to below 10%
- Maintain stocks at one month of sales (2 weeks in December)
- Reduce employee injuries to zero per year

Resources

- Total variable manufacturing cost $3 million/annum
- Total fixed manufacturing cost $2 million/annum
- 4 CarNob manufacturing machines and IT control system
- 12 Machine operators working in 3 shifts, 3 Supervisors
- 1 Manufacturing Manager and 1 Quality Control Manager
- 1 Machine mechanic plus tools
- Work shop with air control and firefighting systems
- Utilities (electricity, water), chemicals and lubricants
- Allocation (based on head count) of company systems

Activities

- Manufacturing CarNobs safely
- CarNob quality control
- CarNob production planning/coordination with sales
- Stock control
- Coordinate with procurement, ensuring continuous production

Interactions

- Unions
- Authorities regulating conditions for workers
- Machinery supplier and servicer
- Raw Material Suppliers
- Procurement Function
- IT Department

CarNob Ltd: Risk Subject 3
Procurement Function

Targets

- Achieve 5% discount verses benchmarks for $5m/yr of expenditure
- Approve 3 reliable, quality suppliers for all key raw materials
- Agree 70% of demand with secure contracts by year end
- Test new suppliers for 50% of key raw materials by end Sept
- Zero procurement related manufacturing down time
- Increase average payment terms to 6 months for 80% demand

Resources

- 1 Manager, 2 Procurement Clerks and 1 Admin Assistant
- 4 Terminals linked to company IT system
- 4 Office phone systems, 1 mobile phone & running costs
- Open plan office and utilities for 4 work stations
- Allocation (based on head count) of company systems

Activities

- Procure all raw materials and consumable items
- Manage negotiation of fixed and capital items
- Manage procurement related working capital needs
- Manage supplier service & quality of products
- Maintain contingency plans to ensure continuous production
- Gather Market intelligence/procurement trend information

Interactions

- Suppliers
- Production Department
- Sales Department
- Industrial Bodies
- IT Department

III. Identifying Risks: The DOSER Workshop

The value TRAI classification, introduced in the last chapter, describes the key value elements which characterise a risk subject. Describing the risk subject in this way allows a methodical identification of the risks which influence business value to be undertaken. A methodical approach will make it less likely that important threats and opportunities are overlooked. Risk identification takes place in a **DOSER workshop**. This is a structured 'brain storming' session and the letters of the word DOSER reinforce the basic philosophy which underscores the workshop.

> # DOSER
>
> DON'T
>
> OPPOSE,
>
> SUGGEST
>
> EVERY
>
> RISK

DOSER Workshop: Four Key Success Factors

There are four factors which contribute to a successful DOSER workshop:

1. A clear risk evaluation scope: the risk subject and its value TRAI
2. A framework to structure the workshop: the value TRAI

3.   A combination of experienced and diverse participants

4.   The DOSER philosophy: Don't Oppose, Suggest Every Risk

Let us consider each of these points in more detail.

1. A clear risk evaluation scope: the risk subject and its value TRAI

The concept of the risk subject was discussed in the previous chapter. A common challenge faced by brain storming sessions is: how to keep the team focused on the item under review but at the same time encourage 'out of the box' thinking. Each DOSER session addresses this by focusing on a single risk subject. The value TRAI for this risk subject defines which items are included in the scope.

If during the DOSER workshop the scope of the risk subject is unclear this may indicate that the composition of its value TRAI needs reviewing. If some important value elements are found to be missing these can be added to the value TRAI during the session.

2. A framework to structure the workshop: the value TRAI

The risk subject's value TRAI not only helps to clarify scope; it also provides a framework for managing the DOSER workshop. The workshop uses the value elements identified under the four value TRAI categories as prompts in the risk identification process. These value elements were chosen because they are important to the creation, or protection, of business value. Therefore any threats or opportunities which influence these value elements also have the potential to influence business value.

3. A combination of experienced and diverse participants

The objective of a DOSER workshop is to identify every opportunity and threat which has the potential to influence the value of the risk subject. Participants should be selected to provide a combination of relevant and diverse business experience and knowledge.

Some risk exposures are obvious to people involved in the day-to-day activities of the risk subject. They will be able to identify many threats by simply using their experience of what went wrong in the past! They will also have come across potential opportunities which perhaps the business has not had the time or resources to pursue. Therefore the DOSER workshop needs to have people with relevant experience of activities from inside the risk subject.

In addition to this internal expertise it can be useful to stand back from the risk subject and view it as a neutral, independent, observer. External observers tend to be more able to identify any 'not invented here' issues. This can be particularly important when considering risks caused by changes in the external environment. For example, if the risk subject is a sales department the DOSER workshop may benefit from inviting somebody from the procurement and research departments. The former may be aware of potential problems sourcing certain raw materials which could affect product availability; the later may have read about new technology which will allow new functionality to be added to products. Therefore, the inclusion of external participants with diverse backgrounds will increase the likelihood that less obvious threats and opportunities are identified.

Often the output from a workshop can be improved by including participants with some relevant specialist knowledge or experience (e.g. engineering, industry or legal experts). If the risk subject has important interactions with a specific part of the outside world it may also be useful to invite experts who understand the relevant economic and business environment.

For a risk subject which is a small part of a large organisation, suitable 'external' participants may be found in other parts of the same company. This approach can be useful if the activities of the risk subject are confidential or highly sensitive.

4. The DOSER philosophy: Don't Oppose, Suggest Every Risk

A successful DOSER workshop should produce a large number of risk proposals. The intention is to identify as many threats and opportunities as possible in order to reduce the chance that an important risk is overlooked. Therefore, at this early stage, no proposal should be considered irrelevant. Participants should be encouraged to suggest every conceivable opportunity or threat. They should not be criticised for unusual ideas. At a later stage a process of risk prioritisation will be undertaken to filter out less important risks (see the chapters describing the V&LIUMM process).

Organising a DOSER Workshop

The ideal number of participants in a DOSER workshop is between 5 and 8 with up-to 40% sourced from outside the risk subject. Workshops should have a facilitator to keep the team focused on the scope (the value TRAI) and ensure that sufficient time is allocated to each value element. In addition the facilitator encourages full participation of all attendees and prompts the team to identify both threats and opportunities. An important facilitation objective is to ensure that 'quieter' attendees also get an opportunity to contribute. When appropriate the facilitator should reinforce the philosophy behind the workshop; 'Don't Oppose, Suggest Every Risk'.

The DOSER workshop can be made more efficient my providing participants with an advance copy of the risk subject's value TRAI. This gives them an opportunity to prepare and start to consider any potential threats or opportunities which may impact delivery of the value TRAI targets. Depending on the level of preparation and the complexity of the risk subject a DOSER workshop can take between 2 and 4 hours.

During the workshop the value TRAI is used to structure the order of events and risk suggestions from the team will be placed onto flip-charts; using one chart for each of the four value TRAI categories. The targets for the risk subject are listed onto a 'T' flip-chart. The workshop team starts by reviewing these targets. The facilitator introduces each target in turn and encourages a short discussion to ensure that the team understands what each target means for the risk subject. This will familiarise the attendees with the purpose and deliverables of the risk subject and the scope of the risk evaluation. All the risks identified by the team must have the potential to influence the delivery of these targets either positively (for opportunities) or a negatively (for threats).

Following the target familiarisation process the team works through the other three value TRAI categories: resources, activities, and interactions. The names of these categories are used as headings on the remaining three flip-charts. The relevant key value elements are written under the appropriate R, A, or I, category headings.

The DOSER participants write their risk suggestions onto self adhesive labels. The value elements serve as prompts to help them identify threats and opportunities. Threats and opportunities can be distinguished by either using different coloured labels or simply adding a sign to the front of each risk: a '+' for opportunities and a '-' for threats. The labels are then attached to one of the three flip charts next to the appropriate R, A, or I, value element.

If a risk is identified but can not easily be allocated to a value element it can be placed into a 'miscellaneous' pool to be reviewed at the end of the workshop. Sometimes risks in the miscellaneous pool influence value elements which were overlooked during the preparation of the original value TRAI. Alternatively a miscellaneous risk may turn out to have an influence which on further consideration is found to be outside of the scope for this risk subject.

The process of identifying risks and allocating their labels to flip charts should take up-to one hour. The exact timing will depend on the complexity of the risk subject. After the risk labels have been attached the facilitator gathers the team together to review with them the risks associated with each value element. Each value element is addressed in turn to try and identify any duplication or overlaps between the risks identified for it. The objective of the review is to produce a comprehensive list of discrete, but still non-prioritised risks, which have the potential to influence the value of the risk subject.

The information arising from this risk review is documented on the left hand column of a simple risk table. This **DOSER workshop risk table** uses the template illustrated below:

Risk Description*	Risk Causes	Risk Consequences	Targets Influenced		
			1st.	2nd.	3rd.
#1	A B C	A B C			
#2	A B C	A B C			
#3	A B C	A B C			
#4	A B C	A B C			

* Add a '+' for opportunities and a '-' for threats

Table 4: DOSER Workshop Risk Table

When completing this table the team should first reach a consensus on the name and description to be used for each discrete risk. It is possible that a single risk may have been identified by different team members so the team should double check when completing the risk table to eliminate duplication and agree a single title to be used for each unique risk.

Following this the team discusses each risk in turn and identifies the main targets which are influenced by the risk. In some cases only a single target will be influenced when the risk occurs. When more than one target is influenced by a risk the relevant targets should be ranked in terms of the risk's potential value destruction (for threats) or creation (for opportunities) associated with each target. The three targets which are most influenced by the risk are added to the risk table. This process of target ranking is based on the DOSER team's best estimate rather than a detailed or time consuming analysis.

When they are identifying which targets are influenced by threats and opportunities the team will need to consider what are the **causes** and the **consequences** of each risk. The names of any causes and consequences should be added to the appropriate columns in the risk table.

In particular the team should consider whether any of the risks are actually symptoms of more fundamental underlying causes. If we consider the risk 'low employee moral'; this may actually be a symptom which has several underlying causes. These could include for example: 'uncompetitive pay', 'inadequate leadership capability' or 'a poor restaurant facility'.

A careful consideration of the causes of each risk will be used later to identify whether, and how, the occurrence of the risk can be controlled. In the example above it may be difficult to identify clear actions to deal with the general risk described as "poor employee morale". It is much easier to devise an action plan to address the specific underlying causes; uncompetitive pay, inadequate leadership capability, or the poor restaurant facility. The "Don't Oppose Suggest Every Risk" philosophy is emphasised to encourage the team to dig deeper when identifying underlying risk causes. The facilitator can remind the team of a little child who is never satisfied with the first answer to a question and keeps responding with another "but why?"

When identifying targets influenced by each risk the team should also consider the consequences of those risks. Identifying the direct consequences of a risk can often be fairly straight forward but it is important to also consider whether there are any indirect consequences. For example a strike may influence normal production output: this can be considered an obvious or direct consequence. However, the strike may also impact the reputation of the company; it could cause disruptions in other parts of the company or lead to customer dissatisfaction. These are all indirect or 'ultimate' consequences.

It is possible for a single risk to have both negative (threatening) and positive (opportunistic) consequences. For example high local labour costs may be a threat to the cost of production but if the labour is expensive because it is highly trained this may help the company to manufacture better products than its competitors, which could be an opportunity. In such cases an attempt should be made to assess the **net influence** of the risk: will it, on balance, benefit or disadvantage the value of the risk subject.

If there are any 'miscellaneous' risks which were not allocated to specific value TRAI elements these are added to the risk list after the more obvious ones have been dealt with. As mentioned above these unallocated risks may lead to a rethink of the composition of the value TRAI and lead to the addition of a new value element. The value tray is designed to help identify risks; if for some reason a risk is not related to an existing value TRAI element it can still be included in the rest of the evaluation process. For example an important new opportunity may have very little overlap with the existing R A I categories. For such risks the targets they influence are identified and then the same cause/consequence review described above is undertaken.

As the DOSER workshop team reviews the risk suggestions it is possible that additional new risks may be 'discovered' late in the process. These can be reviewed in the same way as the others and added to the risk table. At this stage the objective is to make the list of risks as comprehensive as possible.

After discussing risks to resources, activities and interactions the team should revisit the list of targets. Review all the targets in turn to try and identify any risks which may have been overlooked when considering the other three value TRAI categories.

Strategic Opportunities

Sometimes strategic opportunities can be overlooked by focussing too intensely on risks associated with the resources, activities and interactions of the current business operations. To help avoid this situation, ask questions such as:

- How can the targets be exceeded?
- Is the business in the best location?
- Is the business:
    - Using the most appropriate equipment?
    - Serving the right customers?
    - Producing the right products/services?

Consider the following: If this risk subject is created again from scratch what improvements could we introduce?

Avoid Being Judgemental

Throughout the workshop it is important to avoid being too judgemental – as long as a risk influences one of the key targets in the value TRAI it is within scope and should be added to risk-table. The importance or materiality of these risks will be addressed later.

The Foundations for a Risk Management Database

At the end of a DOSER workshop the team will have produced the first elements needed to create a risk management database. This is a table of risks, their causes, consequences and the main value targets they influence. The list is not in any order and is not prioritised. The next chapter describes the process of taking this raw risk data and prioritising it based on business materiality. That is the purpose of the first part of the V&LIUMM methodology.

IV. Prioritising Material Risks: V&LIUMM Part 1

The previous chapter explained how a basic risk table can be produced from a DOSER workshop. The DOSER approach to initial risk identification can be applied to all risk subjects: jobs, projects, processes, departments, and even companies. Typically a DOSER workshop will identify a large number of potential risks. These need to be prioritised in order to focus management activities on risks which have the greatest potential to influence business value. This is the purpose of the first component of the V&LIUMM process.

V&LIUMM has two components. The first involves the application of the **V&LI** (pronounced 'Valley') formula to prioritise risks and reduce their number to a more manageable level. The second component involves **U**nderstanding the causes and consequences or the material risks, **M**inimising the value exposure from threats and **M**aximising exposure to opportunities (abbreviated to UMM). The application of the V&LI formula to prioritise risks is the subject of this chapter. The UMM component and the design of risk management actions are described in the next chapter.

The V&LI formula is based on the following simple relationship: Value & Likelihood = Importance. This very fundamental formula is the basis for evaluating all risks. It reflects the fact that the Importance of a risk is a combination of its potential influence on business Value and the Likelihood of this happening.

The V&LI formula is used to prioritise the threats and opportunities which have been identified in a DOSER workshop. The approach is the same regardless of the nature of the risk subject. The objective is to come up with a single measurement or 'metric' for each risk which represents both its influence on value and the probability of this occurring. This metric effectively **monetises** the risk: this is the term used when a threat or opportunity is converted into a number reflecting both the likelihood and value of its monetary influence on a business.

V&LI

VALUE & LIKELIHOOD
= IMPORTANCE

The production of a simple risk table using a DOSER workshop was described in the previous chapter. This table is a list of risks, their causes, consequences and the main business targets they influence. This simple list will now be expanded to produce a risk evaluation and management database called the **ExposureTracker**. In its simplest form the ExposureTracker is a table which can be produced using a standard spreadsheet programme. Each line in this table contains information about a single risk which a) describes it and b) is used to manage it. The V&LI columns within the ExposureTracker are illustrated in Table 5.

Risk Subject	Risk Reference #	Risk Title	Value Targets Influenced (The risk's maximum potential influence on value allocated to key business targets)										Value of Influence (total) *	Likelihood of Occurrence	Importance (Value x Likelihood)
			1	2	3	4	5	6	7	8	9	10			
	1														
	2														
	3														

* Positive Values = Opportunities, Negative Values = Threats

Table 5: ExposureTracker (V&LI component)

When the ExposureTracker is being used for more than one risk subject the identity of the risk subject is indicated in the first column. This can simply be an abbreviation or reference code which is then explained using an abbreviation key. This will facilitate sorting the database by risk subjects: a useful option when the database covers several risk subjects and risks are added at different times.

The second column is a unique identifier for the risk: this can simply be based on an ascending series of numbers which are allocated to each risk as it is added to the table.

The Risk Title column of the ExposureTracker contains a brief description of the risk. This is simple and includes key words which can later be used with a database search function. The search function, included with most computer spreadsheets, is useful when adding new risks to large databases: it can be used to check whether a new risk is unique or a duplicate of one which has already been identified. For each risk subject a particular risk title is only used once. However, the same risk can influence more than one risk subject.

The next columns are used to indicate the value targets most influenced by each risk. These targets were identified in the risk table created in the DOSER workshop. For multi risk subject tables the first columns are dedicated to any generic targets used across the organisation. A value is added to the appropriate target column. This is an assessment of that target's share of the total value influenced by the risk (see the section on Value of Influence, below). These values will be used later to identify, for individual targets, the total value exposure from multiple risks.

Value of Influence

For any risk subject the **V** in the V&LI formula is the maximum value which can potentially be influenced by a risk. If the risk is a threat the maximum influence on value will be negative. Conversely an opportunity should positively influence business value. A worst case scenario is used for threats and a best case scenario for opportunities. The probability of these 'scenarios' actually happening is dealt with below.

This maximum influence on value for each risk is written in the 'Value' column of the ExposureTracker. If the risk only affects one target, the total value will be the same as the value in the column for that target. If several targets are influenced and total value is the sum of the values for all the targets.

The value estimates can be added to the database using one of two approaches. The first approach simply uses a numerical estimate of the actual value. For example if there is a risk that a strike will stop production for up to a month, V may be assumed to be the loss of profit due to the strike. The second approach involves selecting the value from a series of predefined value ranges or '**V-Buckets**'. For example the following V-Buckets may be used:

Value Bucket	Definition
V1	Value influence in the range $1-4,999
V2	Value influence in the range $ 5,000-9,999
V3	Value influence in the range $ 10,000-29,999
V4	Value influence in the range $ 30,000-59,999
V5	Value influence in the range $ 60,000-99,999
V6	Value influence in the range $ 100,000- higher

Table 6: Examples of V-Buckets

The highest value bucket, V6 in this example, has as its lower limit a number which is similar to the total value of the risk subject. This example is based on a small risk subject worth about $100,000. Alternatively, if the business is worth $100 million, the thousands above can be substituted by millions. This highest value bucket is used for threats which, if they occur, would eliminate the total value of the risk subject. This highest value bucket is also used to capture opportunities, which potentially double the value of the business.

The selection of the number and ranges of the V-Buckets depends on the size and complexity of the risk subjects under consideration. A very large company may structure its risk evaluation process using a risk subject hierarchy. Here high-level risk subjects like major business divisions will be concerned with higher value decisions and their associated high materiality risks. Lower level risk subjects may find that V-Buckets selected for business at the division level are too big for their more detailed risk evaluation. To cover both extremes a greater number of V-Buckets can be used. The higher value buckets will then be more applicable to the high level risk subjects with the lower value ones finding more application at lower levels in the organisation.

The advantage of the V-Bucket approach is that it is simpler and quicker than trying to assess the exact numerical influence that each risk has on value. Estimating the potential influence a risk has on business value can be subjective. An informed guess by people experienced in the business is normally sufficiently accurate for the process of risk prioritisation. If risk information from several risk subjects is going to be collated, for example in a risk hierarchy, the same approach to registering risk value should be adopted for all the risk subjects involved. If V-buckets are used they should have the same definition for all risks.

For businesses where a numerical value assessment is difficult a qualitative rather than a quantitative approach may be more relevant. For example the following more qualitative definitions may be applied in such situations (Table 7):

Value Bucket	Definition
V1	Insignificant influence on business value
V2	Minor influence on business value
V3	Moderate influence on business value
V4	Major influence on business value
V5	The influence on business value could either destroy (for threats) or double (for opportunities) the business

Table 7: Examples of Qualitative Value Buckets

With this approach it is necessary to define which 'business' is referred to when using the term 'business value'. This could be the value of the company, the value of a business division/department or the value of the risk subject. If the risk information is going to be collated for several risk subjects a high level reference should be used to define business value to ensure consistency. Here the value of the company may be most appropriate (determined by market capitalisation for public companies or by using the company's net value calculated from its most recent balance sheets). In this way all risks in category V5 will have a comparable influence on value, regardless of the risk subject where they are identified.

Once the most appropriate approach for recording V has been selected this column is completed for all the risks identified in the DOSER workshop. If the Total Value column is completed before the values for the individual targets, this total value is divided into the appropriate target columns to indicate how the total value influenced by that risk potentially impacts each target.

Let us consider a simple example to illustrate how targets and value influenced can be added to the Exposure Tracker. Consider the risk of 'Unexpected Flooding' which potentially influences the risk subject: 'Production Department 1 (PD1)'. In this example the value TRAI target 'Production Output' requires the production of 100,000 units per month. In the worst case scenario a flood is expected to reduce production output by 50,000 units per month for a total of 3 months. One influence on value from this risk is therefore the estimated loss of contribution to profit when 50,000 units cannot be produced for 3 months. If each manufactured unit makes a contribution to profit of $5 the influence on value is minus $750,000 (50,000 x the lost $5 contribution to profit x 3 months).

The unexpected flooding may also potentially damage the manufacturing equipment requiring an estimated $200,000 (net of insurance) to repair. Building repairs may also be required which are estimated to cost $50,000. Therefore the total influence on business value from the risk of 'flooding' is $1 million.

This information is presented in the Exposure Tracker as shown below:

Risk Subject	Risk Reference #	Risk Title	Value Targets Influenced (The risk's maximum potential influence on value allocated to key business targets)										Value of Influence (total) *	Likelihood of Occurrence	Importance (Value x Likelihood)
			1 Profit	2 Equipment	3 Buildings	4	5	6	7	8	9	10			
PD1	1	Flood	-$0.75	-$0.20	-$0.05								-$1m		
	2														
	3														

Table 8: Exposure Tracker (V&LI component) – Risk Value Estimates

If a value bucket approach had been used this template would appear as follows:

Risk Subject	Risk Reference #	Risk Title	Value Targets Influenced (The risk's maximum potential influence on value allocated to key business targets)										Value of Influence (total) *	Likelihood of Occurrence	Importance (Value x Likelihood)
			1 Profit	2 Equipment	3 Buildings	4	5	6	7	8	9	10			
PD1	4	Fire	V5	V3	V2						V6				
	5														
	6														

Table 9: Exposure Tracker (V&LI component) – Using V-Buckets

Here the example of a fire in the production area has been evaluated using the V values which were quoted in the V-Bucket definitions given above (e.g. V3 is damage to equipment in the range $10-29,999).

Sometimes it is possible to get distracted by debates about the exact estimates of how much business value is influenced by a risk. The values required here are the best estimates by people who understand the business. They are used to identify which are the important risks in order to ensure the risk management plan is focused and efficient. Therefore the V&LI

team should focus on the 'relative' influence of risks rather than the exact value from a specific loss or opportunity.

Often the best people to carry out the V&LI analysis are those involved in the DOSER workshop. They will know what was intended when the risks were first identified. They are therefore in a good position to quickly estimate the relative maximum potential business value influenced by these risks. Holding a DOSER workshop and a V&LIUMM session adjacent to one another with the same team can be very effective.

Likelihood of Influence

After estimating the potential business value influenced by each risk the likelihood of this happening needs to be assessed. The L part of the V&LI formula is an abbreviation of 'Likelihood'. It describes the likelihood that the value change identified above actually occurs. So, if the risk is a strike and its influence on business value is $100,000 the L for this risk is the probability of a strike of this size occurring. A smaller strike, having a smaller value impact may be considered more likely to happen. Therefore the estimate of L is specific to the size of V.

The likelihood or 'probability' of something occurring can be measured using a continuous scale from zero (it will never happen) to 1 (it will definitely happen and now). The probability of something occurring must specify the time involved, for example, one year. Therefore if a risk exposure has a 50% chance of occurring in the next 12 months its annual probability is 0.5.

As with V the process of allocating likelihood or probability can be simplified using a predetermined set of Likelihood ranges or 'L-buckets'.

Then it is only necessary to identify which Likelihood 'bucket' a particular threat or opportunity belongs in.

Consider the following five L-buckets. A risk has:

L1)   a 50% Likelihood of occurring in the next 20 years

L2)   a 50% Likelihood of occurring in the next 10 years

L3)   a 50% Likelihood of occurring in the next 3 years

L4)   a 50% Likelihood of occurring in the next year

L5)   a 50% Likelihood of occurring in the next 6 months

By using this approach the V&LIUMM team simply has to decide the highest L-Bucket which most accurately reflects the likelihood of the threat or opportunity occurring. If the L-bucket approach is used the bucket reference (L1-5) is added into the L column. Otherwise a numerical probability from zero to 1 can be used. If risk information from several risk subjects is going to be collated, for example, in a risk hierarchy, the same approach to registering risk Likelihood should be adopted for all the risk subjects involved. If L-buckets are used they should have the same definition for all risks.

As with the value categories it is also possible to use a more qualitative approach to defining probability rather than a clear-cut numerical approach. In such a case the L-buckets might have the following definitions:

L1)   Likely to happen in the next 30 years

L2)   Likely to happen in the next 15 years

L3)   Likely to happen in the next 5 years

L4)   Likely to happen in the next 3 years

L5)   Likely to happen in the next year

The choice of definitions and the number of L-Buckets will depend on the nature of the business, the size of the risk exposure and the experience of the team doing the evaluation.

Risk Importance

The next column in the ExposureTracker is the importance or 'I' column. It is possible to prepare this column so that it simply contains a formula. This formula can take the content of the V column and multiply it by the probability in the L column. The product of this formula is then displayed in the 'I' column.

If a V-Bucket range was used to indicate influence on value the mid-point of this range can be used when calculating the importance, I. This can be built into the 'I' formula using a look-up function. Likewise, if an L-Bucket approach was used a simple look-up formula can also be used to calculate I (e.g. 'if the cell in column L = L1 multiply the number in column V by 0.75' etc.).

An even simpler approach can be adopted when buckets have been used for both V- and L- columns. Each bucket has a number; V1, V2, V3 etc and L1, L2, L3, etc. These numbers can the simply be multiplied to produce an empirical indication of comparative risk importance.

The following table illustrates how the importance rating can then be derived:

V1	x	L1	=	I1
V1	x	L2	=	I2
V2	x	L1	=	I2
V2	x	L2	=	I4
V3	x	L1	=	I3
V3	x	L2	=	I6
V3	x	L3	=	I9
V4	x	L1	=	I4
V4	x	L2	=	I8
V4	x	L3	=	I12
V4	x	L4	=	I16
V5	x	L1	=	I5
V5	x	L2	=	I10
V5	x	L3	=	I15
V5	x	L4	=	I20
V5	x	L5	=	I25
Etc				

Risk Prioritisation

The risk Importance column can now be used to prioritize the opportunities and threats. The relative priority will be used to decide which risks should receive more detailed evaluation. Not all threats and opportunities are significant or 'material' to business value. It is important to avoid spending time and resources evaluating insignificant risks.

The ranking can be carried out by sorting the Exposure Tracker using the numbers in the 'Importance' column as the basis for sorting. Most spreadsheet programmes have a simple-to-use sorting function. This will sort the list, placing the most material opportunities at one end of the table and the most material threats at the other end (since opportunity and threat values have been added with either a positive or negative sign respectively). After sorting the risks it is necessary to decide an importance or materiality cut-off point, one for threats and another for opportunities.

This materiality cut-off point will be used as a basis for deciding which risks to evaluate in more detail. It depends on the nature of the business, the economy and the level of risk detail covered in the DOSER workshop. Typically only about one third of the exposures from a comprehensive DOSER workshop will justify detailed evaluation. To confirm if this is applicable check the risks which fall outside of the top third in terms of importance (both threats and opportunities).

A decision can then be made based on experience in the business: Are any of the threats/opportunities just outside of the top third important enough to justify broadening the selection criteria (to include say 40%, or even 50% of the risks)? Conversely if too many insignificant risks fall inside the range it may need to be tightened to only include, say 25% of the risks. Generally speaking material risks have a potential influence on value which is equal to, or greater than, 5% of total value created or protected in a year by the risk subject.

In addition there may be a few risks identified which have a low probability of occurrence but when they occur could be catastrophic for the business. Typical examples could be a major financial or economic crisis, natural disasters or catastrophic failures of equipment or processes. Such risks should be given an enhanced priority ranking if they are considered serious enough to merit the preparation of a contingency plan. Such catastrophic risks should be included in the 'important' category for risk evaluation and management despite their low probability of occurrence.

At the end of V&LIUMM part 1 the ExposureTracker includes a list of risks which are ranked in terms of their importance to business value. Those risks which are selected as important will undergo more detailed evaluation and action plans can be designed to manage them. This is the subject of the second part of the V&LIUMM analysis which is described in the next Chapter.

V. Managing Important Risks: V&LIUMM Part 2

The second component of V&LIUMM deals with the management of risks identified as important using the V&LI formula (see the previous chapter). The importance (I) of each risk was calculated by multiplying the likelihood (L) of occurrence by its influence on business value (V). Risk management is based on the same two dimensions; **occurrence likelihood (L)** and **influence on value (V)**.

The DOSER workshop produced a risk-table which included causes and consequences for each risk. In the last chapter this simple risk-table was used as the starting point to create a risk knowledge and management database: the ExposureTracker. The cause and consequence information produced in the DOSER workshop is used to design a risk management plan. For threats the objective of risk management is to minimise both their likelihood (L) of occurrence and any negative influence they have on value (V). Conversely, the objective for opportunities is to maximise both their occurrence and any positive influence they may have on value.

The process undertaken in the second part of V&LIUMM is summarised using the three letters: **UMM**. These letters are an abbreviation of the three objectives which are essential to effective risk management: Understand, **M**inimise, and **M**aximise.

Each risk has a characteristic profile which needs to be **understood** before a risk management plan can be designed. The risk profile describes the causes of the risk and its potential consequences for business value.

U

UNDERSTAND
CAUSES AND
CONSEQUENCES

Sometimes the description of a risk is actually a symptom rather than the cause of its occurrence. Therefore it is important to look deeper and try to identify if there are any **underlying causes**.

To illustrate this consider the example of a strike in a factory. If it occurs the strike will prevent the achievement of the factory's production target. A strike can actually be a symptom of a number of underlying causes. These include: poor industrial relations, inadequate leadership skills or uncompetitive rates of pay. To minimise the likelihood of a strike these underlying causes must be identified and addressed. For example, can relations with employees be improved? Can training be used to develop the leadership skills of management? Can rates of pay be brought more in line with the market or can the differences be better explained to employees?

When a material risk occurs it has consequences for business value. These consequences are either direct or indirect. Direct consequences are generally easier to identify whereas indirect or **ultimate consequences** may be less obvious, particularly if they exert their influence on longer term business value.

To appreciate the distinction between direct and indirect consequences consider the following situation. A factory identifies a threat that the local authorities discover it is discharging contaminated industrial water into a local river. The direct consequence of this is a fine. The indirect consequence is that the public reputation of the company is damaged. Members of the general public will be less inclined to buy products or services from a company which has low regard for the environment. Recruitment of good employees from the local community will also be affected: who wants to work for a local polluter? Often such indirect risk consequences have a longer term influence on business value compared with more obvious direct ones.

A **M**inimisation/**M**aximisation approach is adopted to manage the risk causes and consequences. This approach is dependent on whether the risk is a threat or an opportunity. By definition a threat will have a net negative influence on business value: this negative influence must be minimised. Conversely opportunities have a net positive influence which must be maximised.

When the causes of a risk are understood this information is used to determine if, and how, the occurrence of the risk can be modified. With threats the first risk management goal is

MM

MINIMISE THREATS

MAXIMISE OPPORTUNITIES

to minimise the likelihood of occurrence. With opportunities the first risk management goal is to maximise the likelihood of occurrence.

It is not always possible and sometimes not even desirable to change the likelihood of a risk occurring. In these situations the management of risks focuses on their consequences on business value. For threats the second risk management goal is to minimise any risk consequences which destroy value. For opportunities the second risk management goal is to maximise any consequences which increase value.

These two approaches can be summarised as follows:

Applying UMM to undesirable Threats:

- Understand the risk profile (causes and consequences)
- Minimise likelihood of occurrence (by addressing the causes)
- Minimise influence on value (by addressing the consequences)

Applying UMM to desirable Opportunities:

- Understand the risk profile (causes and consequences)
- Maximise likelihood of occurrence (by addressing the causes)
- Maximise influence on value (by addressing the consequences)

The Three Strategies for Managing Risks

Using the UMM approach leads to three different kinds of strategy for managing risks. The exact choice will depend on the size and nature of the risk:

- *STRATEGY 1: Accepted Threats or Opportunities*

  No risk management activities other than monitoring for changes in the likelihood of occurrence or the potential influence on value

- *STRATEGY 2: Undesirable and Unacceptable Threats*

  Minimise likelihood of occurrence & minimise influence on value

- *STRATEGY 3: Desirable Opportunities*

  Maximise likelihood of occurrence & maximise impact on value

For each important risk identified in the ExposureTracker one of these three approaches is selected. These will now be described in more detail.

Strategy 1: Accepted Threats or Opportunities

Why doesn't a business simply try to eliminate every threat and take advantage of every opportunity? Using limited business resources to manage low materiality risks is inefficient. In is better to invest time and money in the management of risks identified as material to the business. Less significant risks are therefore simply monitored and action is only taken if their likelihood or materiality increases. These low importance risks were identified in the first part of V&LIUMM using the V&LI formula.

Risk Acceptance on Economic Grounds

In addition to accepting exposures identified as unimportant a business may make a conscious decision not to actively manage certain material risks. Risks can fall into this category when risk management options are excessively expensive compared with the size of the business. This happens when the effort required to manage a threat is comparable with, or exceeds, its potential to destroy value. Likewise the cost required to take advantage of the opportunity may be comparable with, or exceed, the maximum value it can generate. This is described as risk acceptance on economic grounds: management of these risks is not economically justified.

To illustrate how a threat may be which is too expensive to realistically manage, consider the following simple farming example. A valuable crop may be destroyed if a freak storm occurs just prior to harvesting. It is possible to reduce the potential impact of a storm by installing protective transparent coverings over the field. However, the cost and inconvenience of doing this may be worse than the financial losses from an unsuccessful harvest. Therefore the farmer accepts the risk in the full knowledge that sometimes a freak storm will damage the harvest.

In another example a business has a very profitable product line which it produces on an old piece of equipment. There is a material risk that the old machine will break down but the cost of repairing this obsolete equipment is too expensive. In addition, the required spare parts and the relevant maintenance expertise are not economically available. Therefore a risk acceptance strategy is adopted which involves simply running the machine until it stops. The business accepts the risk but monitors the process to ensure products are manufactured within specification and the production operation is safe.

In both examples there is no net economic benefit from actively managing the occurrence or consequence of the risks. They are consciously accepted by management.

Risk Acceptance Desired by Shareholders

There are also situations when modifying a risk is fundamentally not desired by the shareholders in a business.

A) Shareholders Invest to get Exposure to a specific Risk

Such a situation can exist where the core component of a company's business is a single kind of commodity, for example, gold mining. Some shareholders buy shares in gold mining companies because they want exposure to changes in the price of gold. They expect the price of gold to increase. They hold the view that when gold prices increase the company share price will also increase. If this is their reason for buying the shares they will not want the gold mining company to engage in risk management activities which might reduce the link between the price of gold and the company's profit.

The company's management may, however, decide that the risk of a decrease in the gold price is unacceptable. To eliminate this risk they make advanced sales of the company's future gold production using 'futures' contracts. These effectively lock-in prices for fixed quantities of gold to be delivered at a fixed date in the future. This ensures a 'locked-in' sales price which avoids the exposure to an unexpected gold price decrease but also prevents the company benefiting from any unexpected increase in the price for gold for this part of its production.

The shareholders may have bought shares in the company because they believe a major war or period of international economic instability will occur which could increase gold prices. If their prediction is correct they will expect the company's profit to increase because gold is its core product. The company cannot, however, increase its sales price because this has been locked-in using the futures contracts. If the price upturn was not factored into the futures contract price the deliveries will be made at lower prices than the spot market price at the time of delivery. An opportunity to 'cash-in' on the surge in gold prices has been lost.

If the shareholders do not know about the company's policy of managing future price risk by using hedging instruments they will be disappointed. The increase in gold prices will fail to deliver the increase in profits they expect.

This example demonstrates the need to understand the risk 'appetite' of the shareholders in a business. Management must not manage away a risk the shareholders actually desire exposure to.

B) Shareholders Invest as Part of a Risk Portfolio

Another example of risk acceptance can arise when shareholders buy shares in a company as part of a balanced share portfolio. The shareholder designs the portfolio to reduce exposure to negative events occurring in a single company or industry. The shareholder may, for example, have a portfolio containing both oil exploration shares and petrochemicals manufacturing shares. These two types of shares can be described as countercyclical. When oil prices go up the profits of petrochemical companies decrease: when oil prices go down petrochemicals companies make bigger profits.

The investor's objective is to reduce the number and severity of peaks and troughs in individual share prices. This is achieved by holding countercyclical shares where the prices tend to move in opposite directions. They are looking to benefit from an overall improvement in the total economy without having to worry about the ups and downs of individual companies or industries.

This is a form of investor risk management: the investment is spread over several companies to balance and reduce exposure. It works well as long as each company's shares respond as predicted by its core market. Problems arise when management alters the company's normal exposure to its market. Consider, for example, a situation in which management use fixed price sales contracts with customers to avoid the risk of a decrease in its product prices. These contracts benefit the seller when market prices go down. However, this form of risk management has a price: if the market price for the product goes up the customer receives the benefit by having the lower fixed price. Elimination of downside risk is paid for by giving away upside risk. The removal of its natural linkage with the market price prevents this company's shares functioning as the countercyclical component in an investment portfolio.

Once again this emphasises the importance of understanding the level of risk exposure the shareholders in a company expect. It can help to ask the question: 'Is the main purpose of this risk subject to maximise its own profit or does it exist to balance the risks within a bigger portfolio of businesses'. This can be particularly important when the risk subject is just one business within a conglomerate.

Monitoring Accepted Risks

Monitoring systems are used with accepted risks in order to quickly identify if the risk exposure starts to move outside a predetermined 'accepted' range. The owners of a business may only wish to be exposed to a risk while its impact stays within this range. The accepted range can be described as the owners' risk comfort zone and monitoring is designed to provide an early warning that the exposure is moving outside of this zone. When this happens, risk management actions which have been pre-agreed with the owners are initiated.

For example, the shareowners in an oil company may accept or even desire exposure to oil price volatility but only as long as this stays within a certain range. Once the price of oil moves out of this range, and particularly if it moves below the bottom end of the range, they may expect management to take actions to mitigate the negative impact. 'Paper' hedges, like futures and options, provide one risk management mechanism. Alternatively 'physical' hedges can be used like adapting oil production rates or stock levels to reduce the negative impact of unfavourable market price movements. As long as oil prices move within the predetermined range the price exposure risk is accepted by the shareholders. As soon as monitoring mechanisms indicate prices are moving outside of the range the mitigating mechanisms are triggered.

Strategy 2: Undesirable and unacceptable threats

Minimise likelihood of occurrence & **M**inimise negative influence on value

Risk management activities are designed to address one of these two objectives. The ultimate outcome of occurrence minimisation is to prevent the threat from happening. To be meaningful this outcome also needs to be cost effective: the solution must not cost more than the potential damage resulting from the threat. The causes of the threat, especially any less obvious underlying causes, must be identified in order to understand how its likelihood can be minimised.

If, after addressing its causes, there is still a chance that the risk could occur, its potential to influence business value must also be minimised. For a threat this second risk management objective requires an understanding of any consequences it has on the creation or protection of value. These are used to design suitable mitigation actions which eliminate or at least reduce the negative value influence arising from the threat.

Strategy 3: Desirable Opportunities

Maximise likelihood of occurrence & Maximise positive influence on value

For opportunities a successful outcome of the first risk management objective is to cause the opportunity to actually happen. Once again, for this occurrence to be worthwhile the potential benefit must be more than the cost of causing it to happen.

The second risk management objective is to maximise the potential value to the business once the opportunity occurs. Appropriate activities to maximise the value derived are undertaken whenever there is a reasonable chance that the opportunity will happen (even if the actual likelihood of occurrence cannot be accelerated by management action).

Applying the Risk Management Strategies

Let us now consider how these different strategies for managing risks can be decided in practice.

Decision 1: Decide if the risk exposure should be accepted

Before investing resources in the design and implementation of risk management activities identify whether any of the risks can be defined as accepted and therefore simply need to be monitored.

Accepted material risks fall into one of the following 3 categories:

I.   Owners desire or expect exposure to a risk

II.   Owners do not want to take advantage of an opportunity

III.   The cost of risk management exceeds the potential benefit

Let us consider these three categories in more detail:

I. Owners desire or expect exposure to a risk

The example of a gold mining company was mentioned above. The shareholders specifically desired exposure to changes in the price of gold. This often applies where the core business of a company involves a traded commodity. Examples include; rare metals, oil, gas and energy, gems, agricultural products or real estate. If investors buy shares in the company to get exposure to these commodity prices they may not want this to be 'managed' away. Therefore it is important to have a clear understanding of what the owners of the company want it to be exposed to. Their preferences are used to identify which risk exposures should be accepted and therefore simply monitored.

If owners only wish to be exposed to price changes within a specific range this is noted and monitoring systems designed to give an early warning when prices are predicted to move outside of this range. These monitoring systems are designed to trigger contingency plans which address the price movements in the same way as for undesired threats or desired opportunities (see below).

II. Owners do not want to take advantage of an opportunity

Companies have limited resources. They cannot take advantage of every opportunity that arises. This may be due to limits on the availability of cash, production capacity or staff/systems capability. For this reason many companies have boundaries which limit their business scope. These are sometimes formally specified in the company's incorporation documents.

For example, a UK company manufacturing swimming costumes may be limited to business in 'sports apparel' by its Memorandum of Association. This prevents it from becoming involved in unrelated businesses. Demand for swimming costumes is seasonal and in the UK the swimming season can be short. Management may decide that umbrella manufacturing is a good countercyclical business opportunity. The demand for swimming costumes decreases with the onset of the rainy season and this is exactly the time when demand for umbrellas improves.

The shareholders may consider that manufacturing umbrellas is outside the core competences of the company. They would prefer the company to focus on clothing manufacture where it already has considerable expertise.

Therefore prior to considering such 'new' opportunities management must understand whether the owners want 'their' business to participate in them. The Memorandum of Association may give some insight but if in doubt obtain the opinion of the owners directly.

The risk involved with developing a new market opportunity is reduced if a company has the appropriate expertise in: the market, its products or the relevant technology. Therefore a swimming costume manufacturer may have a better chance of success if it introduces a new 'rainwear' line of sports apparel rather than making umbrellas. The risk is lower because some elements of manufacturing and technology are the same. The marketing and distribution channels also overlap. The opportunity is still countercyclical because people need rain proof sports apparel at times when there is less demand for swimming costumes. This may provide the business owners with a more interesting opportunity.

III. The cost of risk management exceeds the potential benefit

The V&LI formula was used to rank and select risks in terms of their importance. This was based on the premise that risks which are not material do not justify the expense required for active risk management.

Sometimes a decision is taken to not manage a material risk. This may be because the cost involved is too high compared with either the potential loss (for a threat) or the potential gain (for an opportunity).

Consider an example in a production department where there is a threat that a key machine may break down. There are a number of actions which might alter the influence of this risk e.g., through regular maintenance or by keeping key spares in stock. One action is guaranteed to minimise the production loss; the purchase of a second machine. This could be kept standing by 'just-in-case'. For most production operations this contingency (or built-in redundancy) would be just too expensive compared with the potential benefit.

Similar situations exist with opportunities. Consider a French restaurant owner who, following a vacation, has identified an opportunity to open a second restaurant in Cairns, Australia. Although the food would possibly be very successful in Cairns the family business has neither the personnel nor the financial resources to take advantage of this opportunity. A more realistic approach may be to open a second branch nearer to home or to franchise the specialist know-how to an Australian entrepreneur.

In these and similar situations a certain amount of remaining risk exposure is consciously accepted by management.

Decision 2: Decide whether the likelihood of risk occurrence can be changed

The main purpose of decision 1 was to reduce the number of threats and opportunities to a manageable size and eliminate options which cannot be economically pursued.

The next decision addresses the likelihood of a risk occurring. This is particularly relevant for threats because if a threat can be prevented from occurring it is not necessary to expend resources on the management of its consequences. If its prevention is guaranteed, there will be no consequences.

The causes for each risk were identified in the DOSER workshop. For a specific risk consider each cause in turn: what action is necessary to either stop the occurrence (if the risk is a threat) or make sure it happens (for an opportunity)? The ideal solution for a threat is to stop it completely but it may only be possible to reduce its likelihood of happening. When considering the action needed to reduce or eliminate the likelihood of occurrence keep in mind the materiality of the threat. Any management action proposed will need to be in proportion to the materiality. If the cost of action is similar to the cost of the potential damage it may be better to place this threat into the economically accepted category, above.

A similar approach is used for opportunities. Using the causes of the opportunity identified from the DOSER workshop identify what would be required to either guarantee the opportunity happens or significantly increase its likelihood. Again keep in mind the materiality of the opportunity: the action to make it happen must cost significantly less than the value created by the opportunity once it happens.

Even when the occurrence of a risk cannot be managed it may still be possible to modify its consequences on the value of the business. This is considered next.

Decision 3: Decide whether the risk's influence on business value can be changed

For Threats

As explained above there is no need to develop a plan to manage the influence of a threat if its occurrence can be prevented with absolute certainty. For all other material threats, where the exposure has not been formally accepted, a plan to manage negative consequences is required. This is sometimes called a risk mitigation plan. It is a plan to mitigate or reduce the negative impact a threat has on the business once it occurs.

The starting point for this plan is the list of consequences produced in the DOSER workshop. The risk subject's value TRAI can provide a useful check-list to make sure no important value consequences of the threat have been overlooked. Each consequence should be considered in turn and a decision made about whether its influence on business value can be economically reduced. As discussed above the cost of reducing a negative consequence must be less than the damage created by the threat.

For example, if the risk is a strike, one way to manage the consequence of a walk out would be to pay a competitor to manufacture the products lost through the strike action. However this could be a very expensive option, it will strengthen the competitor and exacerbate the situation with the work force. The plan for managing a consequence must be in proportion to the potential loss and any additional threats created by the 'solution' must also be carefully evaluated.

For Opportunities

The previous section dealt with a 'damage' minimisation strategy for material threats. Let us now consider how to maximise the positive influence on business value from opportunities.

Even when the occurrence of an opportunity cannot be assured it can be good practice to prepare a plan to maximise value from it 'just-in-case' it happens. This will ensure that preparations are in place if it does occur. These preparations are sometimes referred to as 'up-side' contingencies.

The consequences of the opportunity, identified in the DOSER workshop, are each reviewed. The objective of this review is to identify if there are economic ways of deriving more value from these consequences once the opportunity happens. Consider the example of an opportunity to develop a new product in the R&D department. If the development occurs, does the company have the potential to quickly adapt its production to make the new product? Can marketing literature be quickly produced and distributed? What logistics channels will be needed to deliver the new product? New products are often most profitable in the period before the competition can catch up, therefore accelerating these processes will help the company to make more money for a longer period: the consequences if the opportunity occurs will be maximised.

Summary

The word V&LIUMM is made up from the first letter of the key steps involved in risk prioritisation and management:

V&LIUMM part 1 (V&LI)

Value & Likelihood = Importance

V&LIUMM part 2 (UMM)

Understand the risk causes and consequences

Minimise the occurrence and consequences of threats

Maximise the occurrence and consequences of opportunities

The activities described in this chapter are documented using the ExposureTracker. This is a risk knowledge and management database which provides a structured framework for the control of risk management actions. It is described in the next chapter.

VI. Controlling Risk Management Actions: The ExposureTracker

The ExposureTracker summarises the key characteristics of material risks and can be used with any risk subject. It is also a planning and monitoring framework for documenting and controlling risk management actions. The risks and their key characteristics are identified in DOSER workshops. These risks are prioritised and management actions designed using V&LIUMM methodology. The ExposureTracker captures the outputs from these processes in a standardised way which facilitates the interpretation of risk exposure information from multiple risk subjects.

If it is used with several risk subjects the ExposureTracker helps to ensure a consistent and coordinated approach to the management of their risks. It provides, in one place, an overview of all the important risks identified for the areas it covers. With higher level risk subjects such as companies or their major divisions, the ExposureTracker can focus on the composition and management of strategic business risks. With smaller, more specialised, lower level risk subjects like projects, processes and individual jobs, it can focus more on operational risk management.

Whatever the risk subject the same approach is used:

1. risk identification in a DOSER workshop
2. risk prioritisation and evaluation using V&LIUMM methodology
3. information from a) and b) is documented in the ExposureTracker

When used with multiple risk subjects the ExposureTracker can serve as a central repository of important risk information. If it is used throughout a company, risk information from all risk subjects is collated to generate a holistic risk profile for the organisation. This approach makes use of generic value targets which are defined at the top of the company. These are incorporated, where appropriate, into the value TRAIs of every risk subject. These value TRAIs then provide the framework for the DOSER risk identification workshops. In this way risks which influence generic targets are identified throughout the organisation and can receive more focused attention.

The ultimate level of risk detail or 'granularity' in a corporate ExposureTracker depends upon the size of the smallest risk subjects used to populate it. For example if every job in the company is used as a risk subject the corporate ExposureTracker can be interrogated down to the level of the specific jobs or tasks where risks to generic targets have been identified.

In its simplest form the ExposureTracker has the structure given below. This template can easily be created using off-the-shelf spreadsheet software. Each individual risk identified in a DOSER workshop is entered on a separate line and is given a unique reference number. The V&LI formula is the basis for determining the importance of each risk by multiplying its potential influence on business value by the likelihood of this occurring.

By definition business threats have the potential to destroy value and therefore have a negative sign. Conversely a positive sign indicates the value creating potential of opportunities. The data sorting function of the software can be used to rearrange risks so that the most important threats are at one end of the table and the most important opportunities are at the opposite end. The ExposureTracker template is illustrated on the next page.

Risk Subject	Risk Reference #	Risk Title	Value Targets Influenced (The risk's maximum potential influence on value allocated to key business targets)										Value of Influence (total) *	Likelihood of Occurrence	Importance (Value x Likelihood)
			1	2	3	4	5	6	7	8	9	10			
	1														
	2														
	3														
	4														
	5														
	6														
	7														
	8														
	9														
	10														
	11														

* Positive Values = Opportunities, Negative Values = Threats

Table 10: ExposureTracker (V&LI component)

Risk Subject	Risk Reference #	Cause (Ca) or Consequence (Cons) use a separate line to describe each cause or consequence management action identified for this risk	Risk Management Action a) Minimise occurrence of threats & their negative consequences b) Maximise occurrence of opportunities & their positive consequences c) Monitor occurrence of all risks & their potential to materially influence value	RAP Risk- Accountable Person	Time for delivery
	1				
	2				
	3				
	4				
	5				
	6				
	7				
	8				
	9				
	10				
	11				

Table 11: ExposureTracker (UMM component)

ExposureTracker: Adding Risk Management Actions

After using the V&LI formula to rank risks based on their importance, risk management actions are added for each risk using the guidelines introduced in the previous chapter. These guidelines are summarised below:

Action 1: Decide if the risk exposure should be accepted

Where risks are not material or where the owners of the business have decided to accept exposure to a specific risk; the only management activity is to monitor the risk. If the likelihood of its occurrence or the potential size of its influence on value moves outside pre-determined limits the situation should be reassessed. Based on this reassessment a risk management approach as in 2 or 3 (below) may be substituted.

Action 2: Decide whether the likelihood of risk occurrence can be changed

Identify the causes of material risks. Use these to decide if the likelihood of risk occurrence can be changed. If the occurrence can be changed:

- For threats: identify actions which prevent the occurrence or reduce its likelihood
- For opportunities: identify actions which ensure the opportunity does occur or which increase its likelihood

Action 3: Decide whether the risk's influence on business value can be changed

Identify any material consequences on business value if the risk occurs; consider both direct and indirect consequences. For each consequence prepare an action plan which:

- For threats: minimises their negative influence on value
- For opportunities: maximises the value they can create

Let us now consider how the 3 decisions described above are applied in practice.

Acceptable Risks

Each material risk is reviewed. The first question to consider is whether or not the risk is 'accepted' by the owners of the business? Different reasons for risks being accepted were explained in the previous chapter. The risk management action for accepted risks is simply to monitor them. If there are limits to the risk's acceptability these should also be noted in the Action column.

For example the company may buy fuel oil for power generation and decides to accept the risk of 'changes to the price of fuel' as long as the changes stay within a certain range. If however fuel oil becomes more expensive than the top end of the acceptable range the company may want to start actively managing the risk exposure. For example it may decide to install equipment to generate power using gas or solar energy in order to reduce its demand for fuel oil. Therefore once the prices move outside of the acceptable range the risk starts to be treated like any other unacceptable material threat (see below).

For each risk the person responsible for all management actions (including monitoring) is the Risk Accountable Person (RAP). This person is identified in the RAP column of the ExposureTracker. Only one person is accountable for ensuring that all the actions associated with an individual risk are carried out. Certain specific tasks or sub-actions may be delegated by this person to others who are more qualified to deliver them, however the ultimate responsibility to make sure they deliver their actions stays with the RAP.

For example a production director may be identified as the RAP for a risk that the 'workforce strikes for higher pay'. This RAP may delegate specific 'sub-actions' to the HR manager and to the communications manager. However since the production director is the RAP with ultimate accountability for management of this risk, he or she must make sure the HR and communications managers carry out their tasks correctly and on time.

The timing of the monitoring activities (when monitoring should start and the frequency of any reviews) is identified in the Time column.

Managing the Likelihood of Risk Occurrence

For material risks which are not accepted the first objective of risk management is to change the likelihood that the risk will occur. The approach is different for threats and opportunities.

The risk-tables produced in DOSER workshops identify the causes of each risk. These are used when deciding whether the likelihood of the risk occurring can be influenced or not. In the Action column a separate line is used to describe actions dealing with individual causes, consequences or monitoring activities. Until this point, only one line has been used in the ExposureTracker for each risk. If a risk has several discrete actions this line must now be split so that each action has its own line. To maintain the integrity of the database for future sorting exercises all the other information about a risk is duplicated onto the new lines created for individual actions to manage the same risk.

As explained above one RAP is accountable for all the actions associated with a particular risk. The name of this person is added to the RAP column. As with monitoring, more complex actions may need to be broken down into more specific sub-actions which are carried out by specialists. The RAP maintains overall accountability for ensuring any sub-actions are delivered correctly and on time. Individuals delegated by the RAP to perform specific sub-actions are identified in the text describing the sub-action.

Managing the Consequences Once Risks Occur

When the occurrence of a threat can be prevented with absolute certainty valuable resources do not need to be wasted on managing the consequences since they will not happen. These resources are better invested in dealing with other threats and opportunities. For all other material risks the following approach is followed.

The risk-table produced in the DOSER workshop included information about the consequences of each risk. Actions to control the material consequences of each risk are identified and included in the Action column of the ExposureTracker.

As with risk occurrence, each action to manage a risk consequence is allocated a separate line in the ExposureTracker. The risk consequence management action is described in the Action column. The Risk Accountable Person is identified in the RAP column. Once again any individuals delegated by the RAP to perform specific sub-actions in the action plan are identified in the text used to describe the sub-action. The timetable for delivering the actions is added to the Time column.

Effective Risk Management Action Design Tips

The nature of a particular business and the economic and political environment in which it operates will have a strong impact on the actions required to manage risks. It is therefore impossible to be prescriptive about the exact nature of the individual actions which will be needed. However the following general tips will help to make sure actions are effective and efficient

Tip I: Make sure the owners want the risk to be managed

Risk management resources are limited and therefore it is important to avoid any actions which incur unnecessary cost. The concept that exposure to some risks is actually desired by the owners of a business was explained above. This is found when a business is heavily dependent upon one traded commodity as its main raw material or end product and shareholders invest in the business to get exposure to risks associated with that commodity's price. Do not attempt to manage away the price risk of such items without confirming that this is desired by the business' owners or shareholders.

Understand their risk appetite and only undertake management actions for risks they do not want exposure to.

Tip II: Focus Management Actions on Material Risks

The V&LI formula is used to prioritise risks based on the materiality of their influence on the value of the risk subject. The prioritised list is then used to eliminate unimportant risks. This allows scarce resources to be dedicated to more important threats and opportunities. Monitoring activities should be designed to promptly identify any change in the materiality of risks classified as unimportant. Materiality may increase if there is a change in either the likelihood of the risk occurring or the potential influence it could have on business value. In such situations the materiality of the risk needs to be reassessed and if necessary risk management actions should be put in place.

Tip III: Make Actions Discrete and Specific

Avoid unnecessary complexity when designing risk management actions. Complexity can lead to confusion and a lack of clarity about responsibilities and delivery. Break the risk down into causes and consequences and identify discrete actions to manage these. Dividing each action into appropriate tasks or sub-actions on separate lines on the ExposureTracker is a good discipline to adopt. Complexity can make it more difficult to ascertain what needs to change when the actions are ineffective in managing risk exposure.

Tip IV: Action Delivery Must be Easily Measurable

Try to avoid risk management actions where delivery depends on a highly subjective judgement like somebody's view or opinion. Identify delivery metrics which are quantifiable and easy to measure. Consider, for example, a risk identified as 'high staff turnover'. A target such as; 'increased staff happiness', could be very subjective and difficult to measure. A more quantifiable approach could be based on the use of a questionnaire which asks staff to rank their satisfaction with a range of items provided by their employer on a scale of 1 to 10. Using this approach it would be much easier to set improvement targets and measure if, and when, they are achieved.

Tip V: Management Actions Require Clear Ownership

The successful delivery of any business target requires the clear identification of an individual who is responsible for that delivery. In risk management this delivery is the responsibility of the risk-accountable person or RAP. One person has overall responsibility for the management of one risk. If the risk management activities are then delegated to several people the RAP remains accountable overall for that risk and must ensure that the others deliver their appropriate actions at the correct time. The RAP must also monitor the risk management actions. If the actions are not working the RAP is the person who ensures corrective measures are undertaken. If corrective measures cannot be found it is the RAP who escalates the issue and ensures senior management is aware of the potential consequences for the business.

Tip VI: Give Risk Actions to People Capable of Delivering Them

Risk management actions should be deliverable by those expected to deliver them. The occurrence or the consequences of some risks cannot realistically be controlled. Their control must therefore not be set as a target for risk management. Alternatively, the person identified to deliver a risk control action may not possess the capability, experience or motivation to adequately perform the task. For each risk subject it is the Target Accountable Person (TAP), who selects, for each risk, a risk accountable person (RAP) who must ensure delivery of the management actions. The TAP must select a person to be the RAP who is both capable of delivering the action and willing to accept the responsibility.

Likewise the RAP may delegate certain delivery tasks or sub-actions to specialists. The RAP must also ensure the appropriate capability and willingness of these delegates. Clarity of accountability for the capability of people carrying out actions should help to avoid situations in which actions are not delivered because "X wasn't up-to the job".

Tip VII: Monitor Risk Management Actions

Risk management actions do not always go according to plan. It is therefore important to monitor them and regularly review the risk exposure profile of the business. Corrective interventions should be initiated when delivery is not in accordance with expectations. The ExposureTracker facilitates this process by providing all the necessary information to control business risks in one document. The document must not be completed and then forgotten, it must be reviewed regularly to monitor progress and initiate corrective actions. The risk profile of each risk subject covered by the ExposureTracker must also be reviewed from time to time to identify changes in threats and opportunities which require the risk management activities to be modified.

Examples of Risks in the Exposure Tracker

The value TRAI examples in Chapter 2 have been used to identify some typical opportunities and threats. These have then been used to populate a few lines in a simplified ExposureTracker to demonstrate how it might look. This is shown on the next pages (the target section has been left empty and will be explained in more detail in the next chapter).

Risk Subject	Risk Reference #	Risk Title	Value Targets Influenced (The risk's maximum potential influence on value allocated to key business targets)	Value of Influence (total) *	Likelihood of Occurrence	Importance (Value x Likelihood)
			(see next chapter)			
1. HSE Dept	28	1 Year loss of operating permit due to environmental discharge violations		-$10 m	0.025	-$250,000
2. Buying Dept	52	Buying contract error leads to faulty raw materials & major end user claim		-$10 m	0.025	-$250,000
3. Sales Dept	17	Important salesman is unexpectedly seriously ill (or dies)		-$1.2m	0.15	-$180,000
4. Production	87	10% Improvement in Production process (=50% more profit) **OPPORTUNITY**		+$1m	0.15	+$150,000
5. Strategy	93	Move production to low labour cost region **OPPORTUNITY**		+$2.0m	0.15	+$300,000
6. HR Dept	96	Management/ Unions agree new productivity cooperation **OPPORTUNITY**		+$0.6	0.5	+$300,000

Table 12: ExposureTracker (V&LI component)

Risk Subject	Risk Reference #	Cause (Ca) or Consequence (Cons)	Risk Management Action a) Minimise occurrence of threats & their negative consequences b) Maximise occurrence of opportunities & their positive consequences c) Monitor occurrence of all risks & their potential to materially influence value	RAP Risk- Accountable Person	Time for delivery
1	28	**Ca**: Effluent quality changes within hours	Improve monitoring of effluent quality (change from daily sample testing to hourly on-line testing of effluent)	Prod. Mgr (covers HSE)	Within 1 month
1	28	**Cons**: Bad Relationship with Authorities	Improve relationship with Authorities (from less than 1 meeting/year to regular lunch and learn sessions)	Prod. Mgr	Now
2	52	**Ca 1**: Little involvement of legal in contracts	1. Introduce legally vetted standard templates for all business contracts (including procurement)	CFO (legal issues & procurement)	Within 3 months
2	52	**Ca 2**: No in-coming QC tests	2. Introduce quality checks prior to manufacture for high risk raw materials	CFO (covers Quality Dept)	Within 1 month
3	17	**Ca**: Poor health of staff	Introduce health awareness programme and regular staff health checks	HR Mgr	Now and Annually
3	17	**Cons**: No back-up for key jobs	Introduce staff coverage reviews and job rotation for key positions	HR Mgr	Annually
4	87	**Ca**: Ideas from employees	Develop options, select best & secure finance from Board of Directors	Biz Dev Mgr	3 mnths
5	93	**Ca**: Lower labour costs in other regions	Evaluate options of manufacturing in other regions to present best 3 candidates to the Board of Directors	CEO	6 mnths
6	96	**Ca**: Local labour costs becoming uncompetitive	Negotiate with workers representatives to develop an alternative option to relocation to lower cost region.	CEO	6 mnths

Table 13: ExposureTracker (UMM component)

VII. Risk Hierarchy:
Delegate Targets/Escalate Risks

Every company needs a hierarchy of business targets which cascade down from the board of directors to the most junior employees. They provide direction and ensure all parts of the company are aligned behind the corporate strategy. This hierarchy of targets is exposed at every level to risks which can threaten or enhance the chances of successful delivery. Therefore in addition to its hierarchy of targets the company also has a hierarchy of risks. An efficient way to manage these risks is by integrating risk management into the framework used for target planning and delivery.

Many companies are organised using an entity based hierarchy. Under the board of directors there will be a number of divisions which, depending on the size of the company, may be further divided into departments. Larger, more complex organisations sometimes also have sub-divisions or sub-departments. These divisions and departments are examples of hierarchical entities. The targets of the company cascade down through the hierarchy, becoming increasingly specific or 'granular' as they reach the lower level entities. This cascade of targets continues right down to the jobs of individuals working within each entity. The individual can be thought of as the ultimate entity in a company's business hierarchy. The targets specified for each job inform an individual how he or she is expected to contribute to the delivery of the company's performance and strategy.

Each of these entities or jobs can be defined using a value TRAI. This starts with a set of **T**argets and describes the key **R**esources, **A**ctivities and **I**nteractions needed to deliver these targets. In the world of risk management these entities and jobs are referred to as risk subjects. They are the building blocks of the risk management organisation.

By using a company's existing entity structure for risk management it is possible to eliminate the need for a separate risk organisation. This reduces the cost of risk management and ensures alignment between target delivery and risk identification. The combined approach improves efficiency by focussing the attention of risk management on those risks which are most likely to influence key business targets.

Using this approach value TRAIs can also be prepared for special projects or processes as long as they have targets which are aligned with the company strategy and performance, and the accountability for their delivery is clearly identified within the company's hierarchy. In this way risk management can be totally integrated into all the roles, structures and activities of a company. This integration is important because often the best people to identify the risks to targets are the ones involved in the operational delivery of those targets. Using this approach it is easier to embed risk awareness and risk management as core components of the corporate culture.

Generic and Specific Business Targets

Normally the targets in a risk subject's value TRAI will be a combination of generic and specific targets. The generic targets are determined at a higher level in the organisation and ensure that multiple risk subjects are aligned with a set of common strategic or performance objectives. The specific targets are normally decided between the risk subject's leader (the target accountable person or TAP) and that person's immediate management. They are tailor made to provide specific direction and challenge for the risk subject's unique activities.

Targets have two components: a descriptive **title** and a quantifiable **metric**. The title describes the target in general terms (e.g. improve product availability) and the metric describes exactly what must be delivered (e.g. above 95% availability during the next 12 months). Metrics normally include a time period for the delivery.

To illustrate this, let us consider an example in which a company has identified fixed asset cost reduction as a key strategic objective. The Board of Directors therefore decides to introduce 'fixed asset cost reduction' as a generic target throughout the company. At a lower level in the organisation a department producing widgets receives the qualitative title 'fixed asset cost reduction' as its generic target. A quantifiable metric for this target is then agreed with local management to make it clear exactly what actually needs to be delivered. In this example this could be: 'a 5% cost reduction of new manufacturing equipment, per widget produced, over the next 12 months'.

By adopting this approach the company uses the descriptive title 'fixed asset cost reduction' to align the whole organisation behind its strategic objective. The local teams then get practical guidance on how they can influence the achievement of this objective through the addition of relevant, quantifiable, metrics. The quantifiable metric turns the descriptive title into a more meaningful target which local teams understand and can influence.

When setting targets it is important to avoid ambiguity and confusion. This can occur when teams are given targets they cannot influence or whose delivery is heavily dependent on the activities of another team. In the example used above it is important that the local team is able to influence which new machines are purchased, what price is paid for them, and how they are used.

Although the descriptive title for a generic target remains the same throughout an organisation the quantifiable metric is adapted to be appropriate to the local circumstances and the current economic climate. For example, the potential to reduce the cost of new machines may depend on the balance between supply and demand in the machinery supply market. In a recession a price reduction of 10% may be possible, whereas in a period of growth it may only be realistic to aim for a 2% price reduction.

Targets are normally set each year as part of the company's annual planning process. This is a good time to also review the risks to target delivery. By combining the two an assessment can be made of how realistic the targets are in light of the identified risks. Variances to target delivery can arise from either threats or opportunities. A clear understanding of these is used to estimate the potential downsides and upsides to the annual plan.

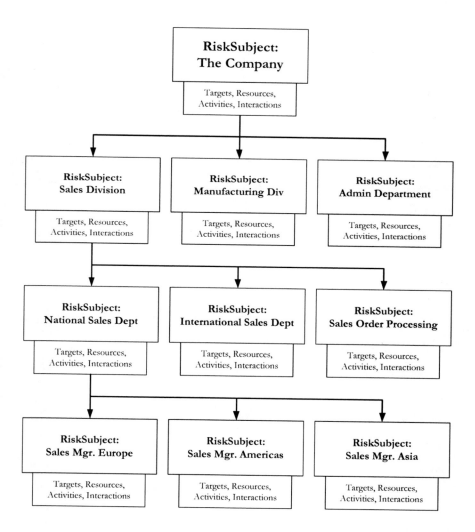

Figure 3: Example of a simple hierarchy of targets,
risk subjects and their value TRAIs

2-Way Information Flow: Targets Down, Risks Up

Let us consider a simple example to illustrate how targets are delegated down and risk information is escalated up using the simple hierarchy illustrated in figure 3.

At the top of the company the board of directors sets high level strategic and performance targets as part of the annual planning process. For example, they decide to adopt the target: 'Increase Export Sales by 20%'. This high level target is then delegated down to the Sales Division. The manager of the Sales Division delegates the same target, without changing it, to the International Sales Department. Within the International Sales Department the individual sales managers each lead a sales team (risk subject) which contributes to the actual delivery of this target through its day-to-day activities.

In the absence of additional clarification there will be confusion between the three sales managers about how much of the 20% increase they should each deliver. For example it is possible that the European Market is already saturated with the company's products whereas Asia is a very promising new growth market. Therefore the International Sales Department manager keeps the generic target's descriptive title 'Increase Export Sales' but allocates a customised 'local' metric which specifies the delivery expected from each individual sales manager. This results in the following distribution of targets:

Chris Duggleby

Sales Manager Europe: Increase Sales in Europe by 10%

Sales Manager Americas: Increase Sales in the Americas by 20%

Sales Manager Asia: Increase Sales in Asia by 50%

This distribution takes into consideration the fact that the company's business in Europe is already much larger than its Asian business, therefore the weighted average of these three targets has been calculated to produce a net 20% growth of the company's total export business.

These targets have been set using a top-down approach. The strategic targets have been delegated down through the company and are customised by management to generate more relevant targets at the lower levels. The risk management process provides the organisation with risk information in the opposite direction. Risks to target delivery at the sales manager level are identified in local DOSER workshops and evaluated using the V&LIUMM methodology. This produces a set of prioritised risks with the potential to influence delivery of the delegated targets. Within this process each sales manager is the Target Accountable Person (TAP) for his or her risk subject. They are the people the company expects to deliver the locally adapted targets.

Let us assume one of the risks identified by the Sales Manager Asia is: 'the risk of non-payment by a new customer'. This TAP decides that the management of this risk is the accountability of the credit control manager. The credit control manager, if he or she agrees, becomes the risk accountable person (RAP) for this risk and has the job of developing a risk management action plan to manage the risk. Typical actions involve reducing the likelihood of occurrence of the risk, for example by only selling to customers who pay in advance. Alternatively it may not be possible to prevent the occurrence of the risk so the credit control manager might recommend taking out export credit insurance offered by the government. Here the credit control manager is managing the negative consequence of this risk, should it actually occur.

Moving up the risk hierarchy to the International Sales Department level it is possible that the sales managers responsible for other regions have identified the same risk. The Asian sales manager may have identified that, if no risk management action is taken, 50% of new Asian sales are at risk from non-payment. The Americas and European managers may have identified a 20% risk to new sales from non-payment in their areas. Moving further up the hierarchy to the Sales Division level the National sales team may also have identified a 5% non-payment risk from all existing and new domestic customers. They consider the risk in their area is lower because they have good intelligence about their customers based on long trading relationships with them.

At both the departmental and divisional levels the combined business at risk in several risk subjects due to non-payment can be estimated. This can then be used to inform the board of directors how much of the total value to be derived from the 20% increase in sales is exposed to credit risk. Clearly, in this example, the drive to increase sales by taking on new customers will result in a higher credit risk. Using this risk information the Board can address the level of resources currently available to the credit control department and determine if they are appropriate in light of the target to increase sales by 20%.

In this way the risks identified by lower level risk subjects are collated and escalated up the risk hierarchy to ensure that high level decision makers are suitably informed about the cumulative negative influence of risks to a high level target. The ExposureTracker provides a formal structure for this collation and escalation process. The information it contains can be used to assess the total influence of risks to generic company targets. The cumulative influence of these risks to high level targets can be described as the company's 'Strategic Risk Exposure'.

Escalating Risks via the ExposureTracker

In the previous chapter a simplified ExposureTracker was introduced. In the illustration on the following pages this has been completed to include the targets section. The generic targets are identified here by adding a 'G' in front of the target number.

Risk Subject	Risk Reference #	Risk Title	Value Targets Influenced (The risk's maximum potential influence on value allocated to key business targets)										Value of Influence (total)	Likelihood of Occurrence	Importance (Value x Likelihood)
			G 1. Increase sales 10%	G 2. Reduce purchases 5%	G 3. No HSE incidents	G 4. No Reputation incidents	G 5. Production costs down 7%	G 6. Production availability >95%	7. Local target Nr. 1	8. Local target Nr. 2	9. Local target Nr. 3	10. Local target Nr. 4			
1. HSE Dept — 28		1 Year loss of operating permit due to environmental discharge violations	-$3 m		-$2 m	-$1m		-$4m	See local copy	See local copy	See local copy	See local copy	-$10 m	0.025	-$250,000
2. Buying Dept — 52		Buying contract error leads to faulty raw materials & major end user claim		-$5m		-$3m		-$2m	See local copy	See local copy	See local copy	See local copy	-$10 m	0.025	-$250,000
3. Sales Dept — 17		Important salesman is unexpectedly seriously ill (or dies)	-$1.2m						See local copy	See local copy	See local copy	See local copy	-$1.2m	0.15	-$180,000
4. Production — 87		10% Improvement in Production process (=50% more profit) **OPPORTUNITY**					+$0.8m	+$0.2m	See local copy	See local copy	See local copy	See local copy	+$1m	0.15	+$150,000
5. Strategy — 93		Move production to low labour cost region **OPPORTUNITY**				+$2m			See local copy	See local copy	See local copy	See local copy	+$2.0m	0.15	+$300,000
6. HR Dept — 96		Management/Unions agree new productivity cooperation **OPPORTUNITY**				+$0.1m	+$0.25m	+$0.25m	See local copy	See local copy	See local copy	See local copy	+$0.6	0.5	+$300,000

Table 14: ExposureTracker (V&LI component)

Risk Subject	Risk Reference #	Cause (Ca) or Consequence (Cons)	Risk Management Action a) Minimise occurrence of threats & their negative consequences b) Maximise occurrence of opportunities & their positive consequences c) Monitor occurrence of all risks & their potential to materially influence value	RAP Risk- Accountable Person	Time for delivery
1	28	**Ca**: Effluent quality changes within hours	Improve monitoring of effluent quality (change from daily sample testing to hourly on-line testing of effluent)	Prod. Mgr (covers HSE)	Within 1 month
1	28	**Cons**: Bad Relationship with Authorities	Improve relationship with Authorities (from less than 1 meetings/year to regular lunch and learn sessions)	Prod. Mgr	Now
2	52	**Ca 1**: Little involvement of legal in contracts	1. Introduce legally vetted standard templates for all business contracts (including procurement)	CFO (legal issues & procurement)	Within 3 months
2	52	**Ca 2**: No in-coming QC tests	2. Introduce quality checks prior to manufacture for high risk raw materials	CFO (covers Quality Dept)	Within 1 month
3	17	**Ca**: Poor health of staff	Introduce health awareness programme and regular staff health checks	HR Mgr	Now and Annually
3	17	**Cons**: No back-up for key jobs	Introduce staff coverage reviews and job rotation for key positions	HR Mgr	Annually
4	87	**Ca**: Ideas from employees	Develop options, select best & secure finance from Board of Directors	Biz Dev Mgr	3 months
5	93	**Ca**: Lower labour costs in other regions	Evaluate options of manufacturing in other regions to present best 3 candidates to the Board of Directors	CEO	6 months
6	96	**Ca**: Local labour costs becoming uncompetitive	Negotiate with workers representatives to develop an alternative option to relocation to lower cost region.	CEO	6 months

Table 15: ExposureTracker (UMM component)

This simple corporate ExposureTracker now includes information about 6 generic targets. Four of the target columns have been left empty because they are used for specific targets applicable to the activities of the individual risk subjects. In this example the risk subjects also have local ExposureTrackers where the influences of risks on the delivery of locally specified targets are described in more detail.

The sample illustrated here only includes one sheet of risks although in reality a company will have considerably more. However these few risks demonstrate how the ExposureTracker can be used to collate risk information from all parts of an organisation and estimate their influence on strategic targets. With a large number of entries the spreadsheet's sort function can be used to sort this risk information so that all the risks influencing a specific target can be grouped together.

Caution is recommended when dealing with the values in the ExposureTracker. The use of hard numbers can sometimes give a misleading view of accuracy. The ExposureTracker is based on informed estimates and can therefore be a useful guide. If more accuracy about a particular risk or risk group is required a more rigorous and detailed analysis should be undertaken. Obviously estimates do not become more accurate when they are combined. Therefore the cumulative information from the ExposureTracker should be taken as an indication of the relative influence of risks on the delivery of a strategic target. This can be used to prioritise further evaluation work and identify corporate level risk management actions.

Corporate level risk management actions can involve restructuring or transformation projects. These solutions may require material investment and could expose the company to other risks. Therefore the solutions themselves need to be thoroughly evaluated both economically and from a risk perspective. The application of risk evaluation information to major strategic changes and transformation projects is discussed in the next chapters.

Non-classical Organisational Hierarchies

Not all organisations are structured using a classical entity based hierarchy. Sometimes a functional or process based organisational model is used. As with entity based hierarchies the risk reporting and tracking system in non-classical structures can usually be combined with the system used for the annual planning and target setting. The same organisational units which these companies use for setting targets can also be used as risk subjects for risk identification purposes. This means that risk management can "piggy-back" onto these structures allowing it to use the existing planning and reporting processes and their information pathways.

The corporate ExposureTracker approach to combining risk information can be adapted to very flat organisational models. These structures may need a larger number of high-level strategic and performance targets to ensure all employees are aligned. These same targets then become the generic targets for the risk evaluation process. If an enterprise is driven using a set of corporate values these can be used as part of the generic targets. In this situation the risk evaluation process looks for risks to the achievement of these corporate values. At the corporate level the risks to achieving these values can then be combined in the way described above for generic targets.

The evaluation of risks for process or project based organisations is dealt with more fully in the chapters covering these subjects.

Ultimate Risk Management Building Blocks: Jobs

All organisational models have one thing in common; they all need people. Therefore the most granular entity in an organisation is normally the job. Any job can be a risk subject. Rather than defining each entity, function, process or project as a risk subject an alternative approach is to structure the risk hierarchy around jobs. Each entity, function, process or project will have a leader and the activities managed by that leader can be used to define the scope of the risk subject. The identification of the Target Accountable Person or TAP for the risk subject is then easy: it is the holder of the job. The resources, activities and interactions are those needed by the activities managed by this TAP.

This means that a risk management organisation can be created based exclusively on jobs rather than using classical entities or some other organisational unit. Using this approach every job in the organisation becomes a risk subject. There is no need for additional risk subjects when new entities, projects, or processes are created, because they will invariably be part of somebody's job. The advantage of this approach is that it makes it very clear that risk management is the responsibility of everybody in the organisation

One aspect of this approach requires special attention: people can change their jobs. Therefore the risk subject should be defined as the job, not the person. If the person moves away the activities covered by the job will usually remain: the job will simply have another incumbent. For situations in which people change jobs there is a special variant of the value TRAI called the t-TRAI. This deals with jobs undergoing transition (hence the extra t) and will be explained in more detail in the chapter on job risk.

This is an important tool for assessing risks associated with the Management of Change (MOC).

All the risk management processes described here can be easily applied or adapted to a job based risk management hierarchy. Each employee is expected to identify the risks applicable to the activities involved with their job (a normal expectation for a TAP). If the job is a relatively junior position the person can agree a simple value TRAI together with their supervisor. This can form part of the annual performance target setting and appraisal process. Once the value TRAI is identified the person can perform a simplified DOSER process to identify risks to the delivery of the job's targets. If the employee does not have anybody working for them a simplified DOSER team might include the person's supervisor, close colleagues (perhaps those performing similar tasks) and perhaps a mentor or HR specialist.

Higher in the company DOSER workshops for leadership jobs can include the team reporting directly to a job incumbent together with any relevant specialists or peers from inside the organisation. Depending on the nature of the activities outside experts may also be considered, e.g. legal experts or technical/specialist consultants. If the incumbent leads a business entity, this process can be identical to the entity risk evaluation described earlier.

Each employee manages his or her own local ExposureTracker and all important risk information is collated using the corporate ExposureTracker. This allows a high-level collated view of all the risks associated with corporate generic targets. As explained above these generic targets are typically cascaded down to all employees. For example, generic targets like 'working safely', 'ethical conduct' or 'minimising cost' may equally be applicable to every job in an organisation.

When a manager is responsible for several other employees (or 'reports'); each will have his or her own ExposureTracker. The manager's own risk evaluation process will need to take into account input from the ExposureTrackers prepared by each employee. For example, a divisional level manager may be responsible for an accountant and a personnel supervisor. The most material risks, identified by these two jobs, will also feature in the ExposureTracker of the divisional manager. For example the accountant may identify an accounting systems failure as the biggest risk in his or her area. This will also be material at the divisional manager's level. The personnel supervisor's biggest risk may be a strike: likewise this would be material at the divisional manager's level. In this way important risks are escalated up the management hierarchy to receive appropriate attention depending on their materiality. Thus risk escalation is equally applicable regardless of whether a company uses classical entities or jobs as the building blocks in its risk management hierarchy.

As the risk management process rises up through the company each DOSER workshop can build on the important risks identified in the lower level risk evaluation processes for the entities or jobs under it. This helps to reduce duplication and encourages the higher level DOSER teams to focus on identifying risks not already identified lower in the organisation.

VIII. Strategic Risks: Strategy SWEAT Analysis

After a risk subject has undergone a risk evaluation, it is often worth reassessing whether the original resources, activities and interactions are still appropriate for the delivery of the targets. The threats and opportunities identified in the risk evaluation process and the actions needed to manage them may be better addressed with a different mix of resources, activities and interactions. Risk evaluation can sometimes even call into question the appropriateness of a risk subject's original targets.

These issues take on strategic relevance when dealing with a high level risk subject like a company. The Board of Directors can use a review of the strategic risks faced by the company as part of a process to reassess the corporation's targets, resources, activities and interactions. One possible outcome of a risk based appraisal of the company strategy is a business transformation project. This will be discussed in more detail in a later chapter.

To carry out a risk based review of strategy a high level value TRAI for the company is required. There are two approaches to creating a company value TRAI. In a 'bottom-up' approach the high level value TRAI is based on the combined inputs of all the value TRAIs below it in the organisation. These are collated, prioritised and the most important ones are selected to produce a composite value TRAI for the whole company. In a 'top-down' approach the company leadership evaluates the company from scratch as if it were a new risk subject. This latter approach does not require any formal input from the value TRAIs of risk subjects lower down the organisation.

The bottom-up approach can be applied where there is an established risk management organisation and the value TRAI classification is used for risk subjects throughout the company. It is the more comprehensive and robust approach. The top-down approach is more suited to companies at an earlier stage in introducing these systems or where the quality of value TRAIs in the organisation is variable. It is less comprehensive but quicker and simpler to implement. This top-down, approach, will be described here.

Prior to the preparation of the company value TRAI one member of the company leadership team is identified as the Target Accountable Person (TAP). The TAP is the person held accountable by the business owners for the delivery of strategic targets: for a company this will normally be the CEO or Managing Director. As with any risk subject, this TAP is also accountable for the risk management process including the preparation of the value TRAI (although, in the case of the CEO, this task may be appropriately delegated).

The company value TRAI is produced using the standard approach described earlier. Up to 10 targets are identified which define how value delivery by the company will be measured (the T in the value TRAI). Normally at the corporate level these targets are approved by the board of directors (on behalf of the shareholders of the company).

To keep the process focused, only the key resources (R), activities (A) and interactions (I) required to deliver these strategic targets are included in the company value TRAI. Up-to 15 resource items, 10 activities and 20 key interactions are typically used for this high level overview. In a relatively simple business even fewer key value elements may be sufficient to capture the important contributors to business value. An example of a company value TRAI is given on the next page.

CARNOB LTD: COMPANY VALUE TRAI

Targets

- One of Europe's top 3 CarNob producers by sales turnover
- Preferred CarNob supplier to at least 2 German Car Makers
- 10% return on sales after all costs deducted
- 20% Return on Capital Employed
- First to Market with CarNob innovations
- Lowest cost producer of high-tech CarNobs (trade assoc. benchmark)
- No 1 for CarNob quality (independent customer survey result)
- 15% of profits re-invested in CarNob research and development

Resources

- Strong Balance Sheet – low debts
- Strong financial delivery track record
- Bavarian Manufacturing Site (Near main customers)
- Leading in-house tech knowledge on CarNobs (53 Patents)
- 4 high-tech CarNob manufacturing extruders
- 60 highly skilled German & long-serving Gastarbeiter staff
- IT: new integrated control system (Production/Sales/Logistics)
- 6 Months stock of raw materials and end products

Activities

- Manufacture high tech CarNobs for Auto industry
- CarNob Research and Development (and Patenting)
- Sales of CarNobs to Auto Industry
- Delivery of CarNobs to Auto Industry (own transport fleet)

Interactions

- All Major Car Manufacturers (all use CarNob type products)
- Regional Authorities (Grants, subsidies, permit to operate)
- CarNob Raw Material producers
- CarNob Manufacturing Equipment Suppliers
- CarNob Technology Association
- Control Systems/IT Developers
- Patent Office
- Unions
- Local Employment Bureau

Figure 4: Example of a Company Value TRAI

After the company value TRAI has been prepared, this is used to structure a DOSER workshop. This workshop identifies the risks to the business (threats and opportunities). In the chapter describing DOSER workshops the value of external participants was stressed. Using diverse and suitably experienced participants helps to identify opportunities and threats which may not be obvious to those involved in the day-to-day business. At the corporate level non-executive directors can plan an important role in this process. For each risk the targets influenced by it are identified together with an estimate of the maximum value of this influence.

For example, consider a flood which is identified as a risk to the following business targets: sales volume, production efficiency, and equipment costs. The influence of this risk on the delivery of value associated with each target is estimated to be:

- Lost production $0.5m
- Lost sales $0.3m
- Damage to equipment $0.2m

These estimated values should be discrete to avoid double counting. In this case the value lost by sales is in addition to the value lost by production (the total contribution lost by not selling product is split between the production and sales departments). For these three targets the total influence on business value associated with the flood is $1 million.

Following the DOSER workshop, the risks are evaluated, prioritised and for each material risk appropriate management actions are identified using V&LIUMM methodology. The output from these processes is documented in an ExposureTracker.

During this evaluation the causes of material risks are identified to help ascertain whether or not their occurrence can be influenced. One key risk management objective is to identify actions which minimise the occurrence of material threats and maximise the occurrence of material opportunities.

Next, the potential consequences of each risk are identified to determine whether or not, and how, they can be influenced. For threats the objective is to minimise any material negative influence on business value. Conversely for opportunities the objective is to maximise any material positive influence on value. Actions are then identified for each risk to deliver the appropriate minimisation/maximisation strategy.

The ExposureTracker describes these risk management actions and any related monitoring activities. The actions to manage each risk are delegated by the TAP to a Risk Accountable Person (RAP) together with a timetable for delivery.

Up to this point the strategic risk management process for the Company is identical to that for any other risk-subject. Having evaluated the threats and opportunities faced by the company one option could be to stop the process here and ensure the risk management actions are implemented, regularly monitored and periodically reviewed.

However, the strategic risk evaluation process creates a further option: a risk based review of company strategy. This starts with the question "Are the current targets, resources, activities and interactions of the company appropriate for the strategic threats and opportunities facing it?" The company's risk profile has now been identified and evaluated. This knowledge creates an opportunity to review whether, by changing the composition of the company and its strategy, it is possible to more effectively manage and take advantage of its risk environment. In effect, the output from the V&LIUMM process can be used to transform the company.

To carry out a risk based review of company strategy three areas require careful consideration:

- the company's current strengths and weaknesses
- the key risks it faces (threats and opportunities)
- the resources, activities and interactions needed to manage the risks

The company's strategic targets can be used to provide a consistent framework during the evaluation of these three areas. This approach is the basis of a strategy SWEAT analysis.

Strategy SWEAT Analysis

A strategy SWEAT analysis is a review of the composition of a company and its risk exposures from a 'strategic targets' perspective. The analysis is structured using the strategic targets. First a review is carried out for each target of the company's strengths and weaknesses, its risk exposures and the actions needed to manage these exposures. Then based on this review the items needed to transform the company are described for each target using a target specific value TRAI. This provides a framework which can then be used in the design of a transformation project.

Strategy Targets from the company value TRAI	**S**trengths of company with regard to target delivery	**W**eaknesses of company with regard to target delivery	**E**xposures Risks which influence this target delivery	**A**ctions proposed to manage these risks	**TRAI** items needed to deliver the actions
Target 1.	1. 2. 3. ...	1. 2. 3. ...	1. 2. 3. ...	1. 2. 3. ...	Target (still OK?) Resources Activities Interactions
Target 2.	1. 2. 3. ...	1. 2. 3. ...	1. 2. 3. ...	1. 2. 3. ...	Target (still OK?) Resources Activities Interactions
Target 3.	1. 2. 3. ...	1. 2. 3. ...	1. 2. 3. ...	1. 2. 3. ...	Target (still OK?) Resources Activities Interactions

Table 16: Template used for a Strategy SWEAT analysis

The Strategy SWEAT analysis starts by listing the original strategic targets of the company down the left hand side of the template. These can be taken directly from the company value TRAI. Then the strategy review team identifies the main strengths and weaknesses of the company in relation to each of these strategic targets.

After the strengths and weaknesses have been identified the risks and associated actions for each of the targets can be added. These are taken straight from the ExposureTracker by sorting it using the appropriate target column as the sort key. If a large number of risks have been identified for a specific target these can be prioritised based on their estimated potential influence on target value (provided under the respective target column in the ExposureTracker). It is important here to ensure opportunities as well as threats are included in the analysis. These are segregated in the ExposureTracker by the difference in the sign of their influence on value.

After the company's strengths, weaknesses, its risk profile and associated actions, have been added to the template, the strategy SWEAT team identifies which additional resources, activities and interactions are required to manage these threats and opportunities. In effect, a series of mini value TRAIs is produced addressing the key management actions needed to deal with those risks which could potentially influence each strategic target. This information is entered under the TRAI headings in the final column of the SWEAT template.

At the end of this analysis the team will have a list of the resources, activities and interactions required to derive maximum value from the threats and opportunities identified for the original set of strategic targets. It is quite possible that through this process the team identifies that the original strategic targets need to be modified and in some cases new strategic targets may be required. For example, a business with an original target 'to expand in the national market' may now decide to introduce a new target 'to identify how to develop an overseas operation' in order to address the risk of over dependence on a stagnating national market.

Where new strategic targets are required, these can either be added to the target list as new targets, or by modifying existing, but now inappropriate, targets.

The tables on the following pages illustrate, for the imaginary CarNob Company, how some of the strengths, weaknesses, risks and actions might appear in a strategy SWEAT template.

Strategy Targets from the company value-TRAI	Strengths of company with regard to target delivery	Weaknesses of company with regard to target delivery
Target 1. To be one of Europe's top 3 CarNob producers by sales turnover	1. Long experience in top 3 2. Financially healthy/strong 3. Sells on quality/technology	1. Can be conservative/not hungry 2. Inflexible production management 3. Can't compete in low cost markets
Target 2. Preferred CarNob supplier to at least 2 German Car Makers	1. German relationships strong 2. Located in southern Germany 3. Culturally close (quality/tech)	1. Weaker relations outside Germany 2. Highly dependent on Germany 3. Over exposure to 2 customers
Target 3. 10% return on sales after all costs deducted	1. Last 10 yrs at this level 2. Best returns in market 3. Focus on quality customers	1. Is return on sales the best measure? 2. Ignores low return, high volume biz 3. Costs high vs. Asian CarNob Co's
Target 4. 20% Return on Capital Employed (ROCE)	1. Investment Efficiency Focus 2. Tight Cash control 3. Good ROCE track record	1. Avoids higher risk investments 2. Poor stock/debtor control 3. Industry trend is to lower returns
Target 5. Be first to Market with CarNob innovations	1. Strong R&D Department 2. Technical innovation history 3. Customers like tech support	1. Like 'tech' solutions not cheap ones 2. Tech costs highest in industry 3. Customers take advantage of us
Target 6. Lowest cost producer of high-tech CarNobs (using trade assoc. benchmark)	1. Most efficient in tech market 2. Favoured by equip producers 3. Versatile production equip	1. Others lead in commodity market 2. We are equip producer guinea pigs 3. Long turnaround times
Target 7. No 1 for CarNob quality (independent customer survey result)	1. Germans like quality control 2. Good QC before dispatch 3. No 1 for 9 years out of 10	1. Asians didn't participate in survey 2. QC can delay urgent deliveries 3. Year before last Polish Co Nr 1!
Target 8. 15% of profits re-invested in CarNob research and development	1. More than competition 2. High-tech CarNob: always 1st 3. 'We are technology led'=plus	1. Used to be greater percentage 2. Asians quickly copy, always Nr 2 3. 'We are technology led!'=minus?

Table 17: CarNob Ltd: Strategy SWEAT analysis - part 1

Strategy Targets from the company value-TRAI	Exposures Risks which influence this target delivery	Actions proposed to manage these risks
Target 1. To be one of Europe's top 3 CarNob producers by sales turnover	1. Asia moving to Quality cars 2. Market becoming global 3. EU sales - an obsolete metric	1. China/India production base 2. Increase sales in US & Asia 3. Use global metrics, segment market
Target 2. Preferred CarNob supplier to at least 2 German Car Makers	1. Germans losing dominance 2. German focus is expensive 3. Reputation as 'expensive'	1. Get closer to non-German majors 2. Develop cheaper volume ranges 3. Counter 'high-cost' image (Media)
Target 3. 10% return on sales after all costs deducted	1. Net Return not 'cost' focus 2. Market trend to high volume 3. Ignoring volume customers	1. Develop a cost per unit metric 2. Introduce high volume range 3. Project: Get our CarNob into Japan
Target 4. 20% Return on Capital Employed (ROCE)	1. ROCE typically lower in Asia 2. Cost control too broad brush 3. Conservative view: 'debt is evil'	1. Adapt ROCE target to markets 2. Intro more granular cost control 3. Increase debt to fund expansion
Target 5. Be first to Market with CarNob innovations	1. CarNob trend 'tech to cheap' 2. Living on past tech successes 3. Tech help ignored by buyers	1. Cost/benefit analysis on all R&D 2. Stop non-paying projects 3. Focus more R&D on lowering cost
Target 6. Lowest cost producer of high-tech CarNobs (trade assoc. benchmark)	1. CarNob trend to 'Low-Tech' 2. Our Low-Tech is higher cost 3. Asian producers: longer runs	1. Project: Low-Tech at Lowest Cost 2. Project: 'Why is Japan Cheaper?' 3. Project: Reduce turnaround time
Target 7. No 1 on CarNob quality (independent customer survey result)	1. High quality becoming norm 2. QC not focused, too slow 3. Are we over testing?	1. Project: ID true quality of Chinese? 2. Improve speed of QC testing 3. ID customer critical QC, stop rest
Target 8. 15% of profits re-invested in CarNob research and development	1. Competition prefer to follow 2. Asian R&D production led 3. 2 tech mgrs near retirement	1. Cost/benefit analysis on all R&D 2. Increase R&D focus on production 3. Review tech dept succession plans

Table 18: CarNob Ltd: Strategy SWEAT analysis - part 2

In this example risk management actions for each strategic target have been taken from the company ExposureTracker. These have been ranked based on their influence on the value associated with the target. In the example only three risks for each target are included. For illustration purposes only one management action for each risk is given. In practice an ExposureTracker will provide much more detailed information allowing a very comprehensive target focused review of the risks and their required management actions.

After populating the template with strengths, weaknesses, risk exposures and their actions the final value TRAI column should be completed. This describes the additional resources, activities and interactions required to carry out risk management actions for each target. These build on existing strengths and compensate for any weaknesses the company currently has. They are incremental to the existing company value TRAI – only items the company additionally needs should be included.

For example if the risk action involves setting up a new production line the TRAI would include: resources like machines, technology, full-time employees; activities like manufacturing, production planning, quality control; and interactions like those with planning authorities, manufacturing licensing authorities, sales and procurement departments etc.

Using the information from its strategy SWEAT analysis the Leadership of CarNob Ltd can revisit each of its original strategic targets in turn.

Let us consider the first strategic target in the table above: 'To be one of Europe's top 3 CarNob producers by sales turnover'. Historically CarNob's business focused on high specification components which are used mainly in quality cars. These cars have traditionally been manufactured in CarNob's home country, Germany. However, there is a growing trend for quality cars to be manufactured in Asia. This is the risk. This 'risk' is identified as a major opportunity which will allow CarNob to increase the value of its business (a reminder that not all risks are threats). The action to address this risk is: 'to evaluate the possibility of setting-up a manufacturing base in China or India'. Therefore from this strategy SWEAT analysis a new strategic target has been developed: 'develop options for an Indian or Chinese manufacturing base'.

Selecting a New Strategic Target from a Range of Options

Sometimes there is more than one option for a new or revised strategic target. In the simple example quoted above the company could consider expanding in either a) India, or b) China. In addition there may be several options for delivering the expansion within each country (e.g. a wholly owned subsidiary, a Joint Venture or a licensing arrangement).

To evaluate the various options the company can set up a business development or transformation evaluation team. At the strategic level these options usually involve projects to either grow or rationalise the business. The team reviews the economic benefits (e.g. NPV, IRR, cash flow modelling) and challenges (e.g. financing constraints) of the various options to help rank them and choose the one which delivers the most value. This review must also include a rigorous risk assessment for each option.

The starting point for carrying out a risk assessment for a business development or rationalisation project is to consider each option to be a risk subject and produce a value-TRAI for it. The objectives of the option are the targets of the value TRAI. The rest of the value TRAI summarises the additional resources, activities and interactions required to deliver the targets for the option. Once the value TRAI for the option has been produced this is used to structure a DOSER workshop to identify risks which are then evaluated using V&LIUMM. The outputs of these are captured in an ExposureTracker which documents the key threats and opportunities for each option and the management actions needed to address them. This approach provides important risk information which complements the standard economic evaluation of the options. The options can then be ranked in terms of both their economic characteristics and their relative risk profile. As with a DOSER workshop it is important to consider including independent and diverse experts when comparing and selecting business development options.

Following this process one of the options is selected as the preferred solution to address the issues facing the relevant strategic target. The simple value TRAI produced for this option then becomes the starting point for the more detailed value TRAI which will be the basis for planning and implementing the project.

At the beginning of this chapter it was mentioned that the strategy SWEAT analysis can lead to changes to the strategic targets of a company. Taking the example of CarNob Ltd the following table illustrates how the original set of targets might be redefined.

Original Strategic Targets (from the company value-TRAI)	New Strategic Targets (derived from the strategy SWEAT analysis)
Target 1. One of Europe's top 3 CarNob producers by sales turnover	**Target 1.** Within 10 years to be one of the top 5 global CarNob producers by relative total profitability and sales turnover, with production in Europe, Asia and the Americas.
Target 2. Preferred CarNob supplier to at least 2 German Car Makers	**Target 2.** Within 5 years to be the preferred CarNob supplier to 5 of the top 10 global Auto manufacturers (by CarNob consumption in $'s)
Target 3. 10% return on sales after all costs deducted	**Target 3.** Within 5 years to be lowest cost producer in all CarNob market segments representing more than 5% of global demand
Target 4. 20% Return on Capital Employed (ROCE)	**Target 4.** 20% Return on Capital Employed (ROCE) in Europe and return levels commensurate with normal practice and available financing in new manufacturing locations.
Target 5. First to Market with CarNob innovations	**Target 5.** First to Market with 'profitable' CarNob innovations
Target 6. Lowest cost producer of high-tech CarNobs (trade assoc. benchmark)	See **Target 3** (above).
Target 7. No 1 on CarNob quality (independent customer survey result)	**Target 6.** 'First quartile' rating within 5 years for Service and Quality using global Customer Feedback Agency (based on top 20 Global CarNob consumers by amount spent).
Target 8. 15% of profits re-invested in CarNob research and development	**Target 7.** 15% of profits re-invested in CarNob cost/benefit focused research and development

Table 19: Strategy SWEAT Analysis – Changes to Strategic Targets

To deliver such a new set of strategic targets several projects will be required. In the CarNob Ltd example this involves a major transformation of the company and its business. The risks to success of such a transformation and each of the individual projects need to be carefully managed. This is the subject of the next chapter.

IX. Transformation Project Risk

The previous chapter described how the evaluation of a company's capability to deal with the risks to its business can lead to a revision of its strategic targets. To deliver the revised strategic targets the company's value TRAI must be amended to include the required changes in resources, activities and interactions. Where these changes are fundamental the management of the company may decide to embark on a transformation project.

Transformation projects can be complex involving several functions, departments or geographical regions or they can be more straightforward, focusing on just one part of a business or one strategic target. Regardless of the level of complexity any project can be subdivided into a series of phases called project life-cycle phases. This phased approach provides a structured framework which facilitates both the management of the project and the management of risks. Project risks can be divided into two broad categories: risk to the successful implementation of the project and risks to the ongoing business while the project is underway.

A typical project can be divided into five life-cycle phases. These are:

1. Decide project purpose and measurable targets

2. Evaluate and compare alternative options

3. Plan, design and prepare resources, activities and interactions

4. Implement, monitor and control the project

5. Transition to normal operations & optimise

Each of these phases can be summarised as follows:

1. **Decide project purpose and measurable targets**: A Transformation Project's purpose is to change an entity from its old value TRAI to a new one. Measurable targets are selected for the project which identify when the necessary changes have been delivered. These project targets reflect the difference in the targets between the old to the new value TRAI.

2. **Evaluate and compare alternative options**: Although one option may appear to stand out it is important to evaluate this against realistic alternatives both economically and from a risk perspective.

3. **Plan, design and prepare resources, activities and interactions**: Early, comprehensive planning can avoid cost and schedule overruns and avoid expensive changes during the implementation phase. It also helps with the early identification of risks which might impact project implementation and the ongoing business operations (business continuity).

4. **Implement, monitor and control the project**: During implementation of the project progress should be monitored against the project targets and appropriate intermediate milestones. Unplanned changes must be carefully controlled otherwise they may lead to increased cost, schedule over-runs and undesirable risks.

5. **Transition to normal operations & optimise**: Where different teams are involved the transition from project to normal operations must be carefully managed to control transition risk. Project team experience should be harnessed before the team is disbanded to optimise the operation of the new organisation.

Sometimes these phases may run in parallel. For example preliminary planning and design work may take place while alternative options are still being evaluated. This can help to accelerate the project implementation. In addition the evaluation of the cost and risks associated with alternatives can sometimes benefit from information obtained during the preliminary planning and design work.

Depending on the scale and complexity of the transformation project the activities in the phases can be further subdivided and managed by expert teams. For example certain design activities may be outsourced to a specialist organisation or some aspects of interaction management may be dealt with by the company's existing communications department. Let us consider each of these phases in more detail.

Step 1: Decide Project Purpose and Measurable Targets

The last chapter described how a strategy SWEAT analysis is used to ascertain whether a company needs to make changes to its strategic targets. If the changes are major the company may decide to undertake a transformation project. At the end of this project the 'new look' company is represented by its new value TRAI. The purpose of the transformation project is to recreate the company to reflect this new value TRAI.

The transformation project will also need its own targets, resources, activities and interactions. This is referred to as the **project t-TRAI**, where the t stands for transition. If we consider the old value TRAI to be point A, and the new value TRAI to be point B, the project t-TRAI is what gets us from A to B. The reason the project resources, activities and interactions exist is to deliver the targets specifically associated with the project. Therefore the project t-TRAI is incremental to the value TRAI required for ongoing business.

This incremental nature of the project t-TRAI is important for risk evaluation. For example the risks which influence resources for a project are usually very different to the ones influencing resources in the ongoing business. If we consider a key resource for the project, the project manager, this role is not required once the project is completed. A completely different set of risks influence the availability of a project manager compared with the availability of a manager in the ongoing business.

One of the main differences between entity value TRAIs and project t-TRAIs is that the latter is transient in nature: it fulfils a temporary purpose. Once this purpose is achieved the project t-TRAI is no longer required by the organisation. Risks to a transient project are typically more short term and immediate in nature. In contrast the risk profile of a business entity typically includes many more longer-term or enduring risks.

Despite the transient nature of a project, the key processes used in risk evaluation are the same regardless of whether the risk subject is a project or an entity. Their individual value TRAIs help to ensure that risks identified are specific to their different targets. These are identified in a DOSER workshop and evaluated using V&LIUMM methodology. In the same way that complex entities can be split into sub-entities for a more detailed risk evaluation, complex projects can be split into discrete smaller projects or by using the project life cycle stages. This allows a more focused evaluation of the risks and helps ensure people with specialist experience and skills are used more efficiently.

Being transient in nature many of the project targets are incremental, reflecting differences between the targets of the old and new entities. For example if the old value TRAI target was to be the number one manufacturer in Germany and the new value TRAI target is to be the number one manufacturer in both Germany and Asia the difference is the Asian manufacturing expansion. The project t-TRAI will therefore have as one of its targets the planning, design, construction and commissioning of the manufacturing expansion in Asia.

In addition to the incremental project targets which are derived from differences in old and new value TRAIs, there will also be some targets which are designed to measure and control project management. Examples of such project management specific targets are:

- Project safety and environmental performance (no accidents)
- Project cost and schedule
- Project economics (e.g. Net Present Value, I.R.R., Payback Time)
- Project finance, incentives and optimisation of tax

Targets may also be based on other local issues which are important to the success of 'this' project. For example, when creating a new Asian Manufacturing Operation the company may also include the following important supplementary targets in the project t-TRAI:

- Select a location which is politically stable, and secure

- Identify a strategically aligned partner (for Joint Ventures)

- Ensure local profits can be repatriated

- Ensure availability of capable local employees

Identifying the most appropriate set of project targets is a skilled process and for companies with less experience in project management an external challenge session with appropriate experts can be invaluable. This helps to avoid some of the obvious project management pitfalls and provides a reality check on whether the intended project targets are realistic. It is important to understand that the targets under consideration here are the targets for the project and not the targets for 'new' company. The latter are defined in the new entity value TRAI, the former are transient targets which ensure the new entity value TRAI is delivered (the review of company targets was discussed in the previous chapter).

Each project target should be measurable. If a target is broad or complex in scope it may need to be split into discrete sub-targets. Sometimes milestones can also be used, which represent important steps to monitor and control progress on the way to achieving the final target.

Step 2: Evaluate and Compare Alternative Options

The main purpose of a transformation project is to create the entity defined by the new value TRAI. This purpose should be the same regardless of which project delivery method is finally selected. However, more than one project delivery option may be capable of achieving this purpose. It is also possible that none of the options identified can perfectly deliver all of the targets defined for the new entity. Each project option may offer different economic advantages or incur different risks (both opportunities and threats). Whenever possible it is worth considering several alternative project options. This will help to ensure adequate discussion, debate and challenge before the optimal solution is selected. In such cases one of the options can be defined as a benchmark against which the others are compared using incremental economic evaluation methodology.

In addition to comparing the economic aspects of different project options (e.g. net present value, internal rate of return or payback time) it is important to consider their comparative risk profiles.

In the previous chapter the use of the strategy SWEAT analysis was described. The application of this, together with a DOSER workshop and V&LIUMM methodology when evaluating strategy options was explained. This approach can also be applied to selecting the best project delivery option. When applied to project options this is called a project SWEAT analysis.

In summary, the project SWEAT analysis considers the strengths and weaknesses of the business in relation to the project targets. A DOSER and V&LIUMM are used to identify risks to delivering the project targets and the risk management actions needed to address these. Finally the additional resources, activities and interactions required to deal with the threats and opportunities associated with each project option are identified and compared. This will give a view of the relative effort required to manage the risks associated with each project option.

Some options may allow the original project targets to be improved further maximising business value (for example, if one option creates a unique opportunity to reduce overhead costs this may allow a new cost reduction target to be added). Any such changes to targets are documented in the project SWEAT template. A typical template is illustrated next.

Project t-TRAI targets	Strengths of company to deliver project target	Weaknesses of company to deliver project target	Exposure to risks created by project option X	Actions required to manage these risks	TRAI items needed to deliver the actions
Target 1.	1. 2. 3.	1. 2. 3.	1. 2. 3.	1. 2. 3.	Targets Resources Activities Interactions
Target 2.	1. 2. 3.	1. 2. 3.	1. 2. 3.	1. 2. 3.	Targets Resources Activities Interactions

Table 20: Project SWEAT template applied to a Project Option

Once the Project SWEAT analysis is completed the project options are compared using: a) economic evaluation methodology, and b) an evaluation of the option's risks together with an estimate of the resources, activities and interactions needed to address the risks. Using this comprehensive approach the option most suited to delivery of the project targets in the prevailing risk environment can be selected.

Step 3: Plan, Design and Prepare Resources, Activities and Interactions

Once a project option has been selected more detailed planning and scheduling can begin. A t-TRAI for the project will have been prepared during the option selection process. The resources, activities and interactions will now need to be defined and planned in more detail and a schedule prepared for their introduction into and, where appropriate, their exit out of the project. In practice each of the project phases; Planning/Design, Implementation and Transition to Normal Operations, can be defined using its own t-TRAI. These can then be used as a basis for structuring the planning, scheduling and risk evaluation for the remaining phases of the project.

Bigger project or project lifecycle phase targets can be broken down into sub-targets and milestones to allow a more detailed measurement of progress against them. After the sub-targets and milestones have been identified the resources, activities and interactions needed to deliver each of them is identified, planned and prepared. These are added to the overall project schedule in order to manage the detailed timing and availability.

After t-TRAIs have been completed for all the key phases in the project a more detailed assessment of the risks relating to each phase can be undertaken. For large or complex projects the activities within certain phases can be further subdivided to allow more focused evaluation of their risks. For example, Planning and Design may be treated as two discrete sub-phases with each having its own t-TRAI.

The dynamic and interactive nature of the different project phases requires particular attention to identify and manage transition risks. For example, communications and handovers between the different project phases must be carefully managed. These are addressed under the interactions category of the t-TRAIs for each phase. Both the interactions with the preceding project phase and those with the subsequent phase must be risk assessed and management actions prepared.

Lack of attention to communication and resourcing during project phase transition can be a significant risk to business value. This is particularly important if the different phases are managed by different teams. For example a project implementation team may be rewarded primarily for project delivery. Their involvement in the preparation of manuals needed for operating any new equipment after project completion may not be defined as a priority in their own targets. This should be rectified and appropriately monitored to ensure they allocate sufficient time and effort to this important area.

Each project phase t-TRAI is used to structure a DOSER workshop and the risks identified are evaluated using V&LIUMM. The actions to control the occurrence of risks and their potential consequences on value are entered into an ExposureTracker. These risk management and monitoring actions can be directly linked into the overall project planning and schedule management system. In this way project risk management is integrated into the general project planning and control process.

Step 4: Implement, Monitor and Control the Project

As soon as a team is in place for project implementation they review the project t-TRAI and the ExposureTracker prepared for their phase of the project during the planning phase. There are three purposes for this. Firstly it familiarises the team with the targets, resources, activities and interactions planned for their phase of the project. Secondly it gives them an informed view of the threats and opportunities they face and what is required to control them. Thirdly it gives them a chance to review the content of both the t-TRAI and the ExposureTracker and, if appropriate, make early interventions. For example, they may consider that project implementation requires additional specialist resources, like an additional engineer or a key piece of equipment.

This initial review and any resultant actions ensure ownership by the implementation team of the targets they are expected to deliver and the activities to manage any risks. It also facilitates a closer working relationship between these new team members and the planning team. This is key to managing phase transition risks which often result from poor communications and coordination between teams involved with consecutive project phases.

Step 5: Transition to Normal Operations & Optimise

The phase transition risks between Implementation and Operations are managed in a similar way to those between Planning and Implementation but with one difference. The t-TRAI and the ExposureTracker prepared for the Operations phase by the project planning team are reviewed by the implementation team prior to being handed over to the operations team.

These items are then reviewed by the operations team and it is good practice for representatives from the project implementation team to also participate in this review.

This approach promotes consistency as the project moves through planning, implementation and operations phases. It also helps to capture learnings from the project implementation phase which may be lost once the project team disbands. For example with a construction project it may have been necessary to make modifications from the original design documentation. It is important in such cases not only to document the changes but also ensure the operations team understand the reasons for them and why alternative solutions were not chosen. Ideally, if the operations team is already in place it is good practice to involve them in the management of change process for significant design alterations which are introduced during the project implementation phase.

One of the early activities of an operations team is to try and optimise the facilities and operations they have taken over. This could involve, for example, merging the new operations team with one which already exists. There may be some other synergies which can be obtained: perhaps older systems will be made redundant or obsolete by the new investment. This process will require the project operations phase t-TRAI and the ExposureTracker to be integrated into equivalent documents used for existing operations. Representatives from the project implementation and planning teams can also support this process, making recommendations and suggestions based on their experience in preparing and implementing the project.

A common criticism of projects is that the teams are sometimes disbanded and moved on to other activities before the operations team has had a chance to benefit from their knowledge and experience. Early completion of the operations phase t-TRAI and ExposureTracker with participation from project staff is one way to mitigate this risk.

Summary

This chapter has dealt with the control of risks through the life-cycle phases of a transformation project using value TRAIs, DOSER workshops, V&LIUMM methodology and ExposureTrackers. This consistent approach helps to embed a risk management culture throughout a company.

The concept of the t-TRAI was introduced. This is a special variant of the value TRAI which addresses incremental changes to value elements as an entity moves from one state to the next. The t-TRAI also includes transient Targets, Resources, Activities and Interactions which are required by or consumed by the project. These transient items will be described in more detail in the following chapters.

When companies undergo transformation projects certain areas of risk require special attention. These projects often involve changes to the way jobs and people are organised and interrelate. They may also involve changes to ongoing business processes or require totally new processes to be introduced. The next two chapters address the management of risks associated with jobs and processes.

X. Job Risk: Static and Changing Jobs

A job can be thought of as one of the most fundamental entities in a business and can be evaluated for risks like any other entity. For each job a value TRAI can be prepared which defines the key items required to create, or protect business value. This value TRAI is then used as the starting point in a risk management process using the tools described in earlier chapters. In this process a DOSER workshop is used to identify risks which are then evaluated using V&LIUMM methodology. An ExposureTracker database is used to capture important risk information and the associated management actions from these processes.

Static Jobs

This standard approach to risk management is well suited to **static** jobs. Static jobs are those which are not currently undergoing major changes like, for example, the replacement of the job holder or a significant redesign of the activities performed by the job. A simple example of a value TRAI for a static job is given on the next page.

CarNob Ltd: Risk Subject Value TRAI
National Sales Representative A

Targets

- Sell 125,000 High Tech CarNobs this year
- Achieve an annual average CarNob price of $20 per unit
- Initiate business with 2 new customers by year end
- Reduce late payers to 10% of total transactions

Resources

- Travel and Expense Budget $20,000/annum
- Lap-top, mobile phone, company credit card,
- Access to company IT system, 1 office terminal & phone
- Share of Sales Office Admin budget $40,000/annum
- 1 leased Car and parking facilities near office
- Office Hot Desk
- Allocation (based on head count) of company systems

Activities

- Selling High-Tech CarNobs to domestic customers
- Visiting Customers to negotiate agreements
- Receiving orders by phone
- Entry of orders into company IT system
- Ensuring timely payment by customers

Interactions

- Existing Customers (5)
- New Customers (3 potential, 1 near to agreement)
- Production Department
- Quality Control Manager
- Accounting Department
- IT Department

Figure 5: Example of a value TRAI for a static job

It is important to note that the value TRAI for a static job describes the position, not the person. It is a summary job description which is prepared to support the identification and evaluation of risks associated with the job.

Jobs in the Hierarchy of Company Risks

Since jobs and the activities they perform are the basic building blocks of any organisation they can provide considerable detail or 'granularity' about the risks an enterprise is exposed to. Using every job to populate a corporate ExposureTracker will ensure that it includes risks from all parts of the organisation. Even high level strategic threats and opportunities will be addressed by assessing the risks to delivery of the targets held by senior executives.

Normally in risk identification every risk subject has a Target Accountable Person or TAP. This is the person responsible for the delivery of a risk subject's targets and for initiating and monitoring its risk evaluation and management process. When the risk subject is a job the TAP is the person doing that job. Since projects and processes normally come under somebody's leadership they will also be included in that person's value TRAI. Therefore using jobs as the basic building block for risk evaluation ensures that risks to projects and processes are also included.

The same 'inclusive' logic applies to entities like departments or divisions. These are under the responsibility of a manager and therefore risks will be addressed via the value TRAI for that manager. If a corporate ExposureTracker is populated by evaluating risks to all jobs in a company it should therefore cover the risks to all the operational entities, projects and processes.

This means that a comprehensive job based corporate risk evaluation process has the potential to cover all the material risks that a company is exposed to. It is not necessary to separately add risks identified for entities, projects and processes. However, when the leaders of these areas carry out risk identification they should involve their teams and other appropriate experts to reduce the likelihood that important risks get overlooked. This can be particularly relevant to projects and processes which can involve a number of specialist skills which are not necessarily held by the leader. For the larger entities, major processes or big projects it is also important to get independent or external input into the risk identification process (usually as invited participants in a DOSER workshop).

Where every job in an organisation is considered a risk subject the company's ExposureTracker is a powerful, comprehensive system for managing corporate risk. Risks are identified from each job and the important ones are fed into the ExposureTracker. The risk management actions given to Risk Accountable People (RAPs) can then be included in the activities section of that person's value TRAI (which can also serve as a summary performance contract). Therefore jobs are the starting point for the risk identification process and are also the key vehicles for managing these risks. Used in this way jobs become fully integrated into a holistic corporate risk management system.

Normally for any entity the TAP is responsible for delegating management of a particular risk to a RAP. As explained above when the risk subject is a job the TAP is the holder of the job. This person can either manage the risk by themselves or elicit help from another person or specialist (a RAP) in order to manage it but as with every risk subject the

TAP still has overall accountability for the risk management process associated with his or her job.

When the job is a management position the job holder or TAP is also responsible for the other jobs reporting to him or her. These 'reports' are TAPs for their individual jobs and the manager is the 'higher level' TAP who oversees them ensuring they deliver their targets and manage their own risks. In this way responsibility for risk management goes up the line to the top of the company with the ultimate TAPs being members of the board of directors. Each director is therefore responsible for both target delivery and risk management in his or her designated area of accountability in the company and must ensure all the people working in that area deliver their targets and manage the risks associated with target delivery.

The close association with accountability for delivering business targets makes the process of using jobs to identify, evaluate and manage risks highly value focused. If all jobs are included in this process risks to the value of the entire organisation's operations, at all locations, should automatically be covered.

Changing Jobs

What happens when jobs change? Some jobs include change as an integral part of the job description. For example a role may require an individual to constantly move to new locations or face new challenges. This can be the case with a project manager in a large organisation. Project managers often need to move from one project to the next and deal with the ensuing changes as an inherent part of their job. These inherent requirements to adapt to, and manage change can be dealt with using the static job value TRAI approach described above. The person in the role is expected to manage risks associated with these changes as part of their normal ongoing job. This is reflected in the value TRAI which will include targets for successfully managing change as well as describing the resources, activities and interactions required for the expected changes.

Another kind of change occurs when the job description (or value TRAI) itself changes. Such changes are commonly associated with business transformation projects. Transformation projects like those introduced in the last chapter may require major changes to several jobs. New 'transition' risks are introduced by such changes which are different to those faced by a static job. To deal with such situations a variant of the value TRAI is applied which helps to highlight these job transition risks. The approach uses a similar tool to the project t-TRAI described in the previous chapter for transitional risks arising from transformation projects. Here the tool is called the job t-TRAI. Again the little t emphasises the transient nature of this value TRAI. The job t-TRAI deals specifically with risks resulting from job transitions and provides the framework for a management of change (MOC) process.

The key value elements involved with changing jobs are identified with using two static value TRAIs for the job (one before and one after the transition) and a job t-TRAI to highlight value elements in transition from the old to the new static value TRAI. The Targets, Resources, Activities and Interactions in the t-TRAI are then used to structure risk identification, evaluation and management by applying the standard risk management tools already introduced.

When implementing a major change project, clear objectives for the transformation must be decided before any detailed job changes can be addressed. The previous chapter explained how, for a transformation project, these objectives are described using the targets category in a project value TRAI. Generally speaking most transformation projects have targets which involve reducing cost and improving performance. This usually means trying to get more output from the same or fewer employees and/or assets. In practice the activities covered by the remaining jobs will need to be redistributed, the capabilities of individuals enhanced and the efficiency of operations improved. Project failure often results from the late identification or inadequate management of risks associated with the transition to the new state.

The remainder of this chapter explains how the risks associated with changing jobs can be managed. Value TRAI's for old and new jobs will be used to describe the static state of the jobs before and after the change. Job t-TRAIs will be introduced which describe the transient value elements (targets, resources, activities and interactions) required to get from the old to the new job. Once a new job exists the t-TRAI will no longer be required. It is only needed for the identification and management of risks associated with the transition.

Management of Risks during a Job Transition

Before implementing an organisational transformation a static value TRAI for every job expected to change is prepared to describe the important value elements of each job.

The content of the value TRAIs for the new jobs will depend on the targets set for transformation project. These targets can be determined using a strategy SWEAT analysis which is a risk based review of the company's strategic targets. They are included in the project value TRAI (introduced in the previous chapter). Often transformation targets involve reductions in employee numbers. This is achieved by eliminating non-essential activities, outsourcing others and redesigning and then reallocating the remainder among fewer employees.

To illustrate the process for managing risks associated with changing jobs consider a simple example in which a single job changes by increasing its activities. The example uses the job of a salesperson working for the imaginary company, CarNob Ltd. The change involves increasing the salesperson's product range from selling low volume, high-tech CarNobs to include additional sales of high volume, commodity (or low-tech) CarNobs. The following pages show simplified versions of the static value TRAIs for this Salesperson's job before and after the change.

CarNob Ltd
Risk Subject Value TRAI
(Before Change)
National Sales Representative A

Targets

- Sell 125,000 High Tech CarNobs this year
- Achieve an annual average CarNob price of $20 per unit
- Initiate business with 2 new customers by year end
- Reduce late payers to 10% of total transactions

Resources

- Travel and Expense Budget $20,000/annum
- Lap-top, mobile phone, company credit card,
- Access to company IT system, 1 office terminal & phone
- Share of Sales Office Admin budget $40,000/annum
- 1 leased Car and parking facilities near office
- Office Hot Desk
- Allocation (based on head count) of company systems

Activities

- Selling High-Tech CarNobs to domestic customers
- Visiting Customers to negotiate agreements
- Receiving orders by phone
- Entry of orders into company IT system
- Ensuring timely payment by customers

Interactions

- Existing Customers (5)
- New Customers (3 potential, 1 near to agreement)
- Production Department
- Quality Control Manager
- Accounting Department
- IT Department

Figure 6: Example of a value TRAI for a static job (before transition)

CarNob Ltd
Risk Subject Value TRAI
(After Change)
National Sales Representative A

Targets

- Sell 125,000 High Tech CarNobs this year
- Sell 500,000 Commodity CarNobs this year
- Achieve an annual average High Tech price of $20 per unit
- Achieve an annual average Commodity price of $14 per unit
- Initiate business with 2 new High Tech customers by year end
- Sell commodities to 5 existing & 2 new customers in 3 months
- Reduce late payers to 10% of total transactions

Resources

- Travel and Expense Budget $30,000/annum
- Lap-top, mobile phone, company credit card,
- Access to company IT system, 1 office terminal & phone
- Share of Sales Office Admin budget $44,000/annum
- 1 leased Car and parking facilities near office
- Office Hot Desk
- Allocation (based on head count) of company systems

Activities

- Selling High-Tech CarNobs to domestic customers
- Selling Commodity CarNobs to domestic customers
- Visiting Customers to negotiate agreements
- Receiving orders by phone
- Entry of orders into company IT system
- Ensuring timely payment by customers

Interactions

- Existing Customers (5)
- New Customers (3 potential, 1 near to agreement)
- Production Department
- Quality Control Manager
- Accounting Department
- IT Department

Figure 7: Example of a value TRAI for a static job (after transition)

Chris Duggleby

A t-TRAI for the job can now be produced for the transition from the old to the new job. This describes the incremental changes necessary to get from the static value-TRAI for the old job to the one for the new job. These changes are either additions or subtractions (indicated by + or − signs). As well as describing the incremental changes using a standard value TRAI format important transition specific TRAI items are also included in the t-TRAI. These may not occur in either the pre-transition or post-transition value TRAIs but are required for the transition itself. The job t-TRAI for this transition is illustrated on the next page.

CARNOB LTD
RISK SUBJECT t-TRAI
NATIONAL SALES REPRESENTATIVE A,

INCREMENTAL TRAI ITEMS

Targets

+ Sell 500,000 Commodity CarNobs this year
+ Achieve an annual average Commodity price of $14 per unit
+ Sell commodities to 5 existing & 2 new customers in 3 months

Resources

+ Travel and Expense Budget $10,000/annum
+ Share of Sales Office Admin budget $4,000/annum

Activities

+ Selling Commodity CarNobs to domestic customers

Interactions

No new interactions (additional commodity sales are to companies already contacted for High Tech CarNobs)

TRANSITION SPECIFIC TRAI ITEMS

Targets

Complete the transition without losing any existing customers.

Resources

20 Employee full time work days

Activities

Training Received:	Features of Commodity CarNobs
	Features of Commodity Market
Training Given:	None

Interactions

Here a Communications Plan is included identifying all customers, their needs/desires, messages to deliver, media to use and how communications effectiveness will be monitored. Interactions with ongoing business activities are also managed (business continuity management).

Transition timing

Here a schedule for achieving each item/milestone is included.

Figure 8: Example of a job t-TRAI

In this example the transition specific activities are expected to require 20 days of the job occupant's time. The time is needed for items like training and customer introductions. This time 'resource' will need to be scheduled and budgeted for, as part of the transition planning.

The best way to identify the transition specific items is to consider which targets, resources, activities and interactions (like communications) will be needed, or consumed, by the transition. These are usually items which cease to be required after the transition is complete. If this job change is part of a broader transformation project the person doing the changing job may be required to provide training for other people. For example another person may be taking over some of the tasks previously included in the job which is changing. In these situations planning and budgeting will be needed for training which is both received and given by the holder of each changing job.

The reason for using a job t-TRAI is that it provides more focus to those elements in the value TRAIs which are actually changing. Threats and opportunities associated with non-changing value elements are normally dealt with as part of the ongoing risk management process using the job's static value TRAI. In the change described here the salesperson will need to learn about new products and new markets. These training activities are therefore highlighted.

Communications are used in nearly every transformation to improve the way the change is perceived by important stakeholders and, where appropriate, encourage their engagement and support. Here a change communications plan is used. All significant communications about changing items should be included in the plan together with a budget and schedule. The cost and timing of communications delivery is then monitored and managed against this plan. It is also important not to overlook or underestimate any risks to business continuity which can be created by a change process. Therefore any interactions the change could have with ongoing business activities must be listed to allow the relevant risks to be addressed in the change-risk management plan.

The t-TRAI for each changing job will be used as the starting point for standard risk identification, evaluation and management processes. By focusing on the items which are expected to change the transition team can avoid being unduly distracted by risks which are totally unrelated to the change process.

After identifying all the 'change' value elements the job t-TRAI is used to structure a DOSER workshop. This follows the standard approach of considering all the TRAI elements in turn and identifying risks which potentially influence them. If a transformation project involves a number of similar job changes it may be more efficient to review these in a multi risk subject DOSER workshop. Ideally the employees occupying the jobs should also be involved in the identification of risks arising from the change. They are often the people with the best understanding of the threats and opportunities associated with their job. Sometimes the confidential or sensitive nature of a proposed transformation prevents the involvement of job incumbents at an early stage in the process. In this case a team of people with relevant experience should participate in the DOSER e.g. managers or supervisors involved with this business area, communications and training experts, HR professionals.

Following the DOSER workshop the risks are evaluated using V&LIUMM methodology and risk management actions captured in an ExposureTracker.

Chris Duggleby

The risk management process for a changing job is illustrated in the flow chart below. This describes how the risks and opportunities associated with a single job transition can be systematically identified, evaluated and managed. The main risk management processes (DOSER, V&LIUMM, and the ExposureTracker) are identical to those introduced for the management of risks in other parts of a company. This consistency of approach supports the introduction and embedding of a holistic risk management culture throughout an organisation.

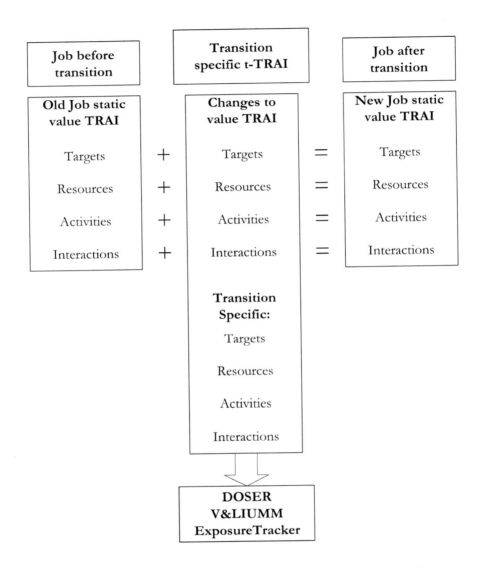

Figure 9: Identification and Management of Risks Associated With a Job Change

Chris Duggleby

Multiple Job Transformations: The Job Trans4Map

The example above dealt with a simple, single job change. What happens when several job changes are required, involving varying degrees of increasing or decreasing activities? What happens if jobs are removed from the organisation or new jobs are created? How are these risks managed?

One of the first challenges in such a reorganisation is to decide exactly how many jobs will be needed and what each should do. Sometimes guidelines for new levels of employee numbers are driven by cost saving targets set by senior management. Alternatively the need to increase workforce efficiency may be based on benchmarking against competitors or other similar organisations. In such cases there may be a predetermined target to reduce headcount by X %. Alternatively management may have decided that certain activities are no longer essential in the new organisation and therefore a plan is needed to eliminate or outsource them.

A systematic approach to such a complex set of changes is needed and this is where the value TRAI helps. By breaking down each job's value elements using the four value TRAI categories the process of combining or eliminating jobs can be systematically approached. This same structure also provides a framework to identify and manage job related 'change' risks which can arise during a transformation project.

Let us consider how this works in practice. Prior to a re-organisation project a static value TRAI is required for every job that is likely to change. The design of the new organisation will be based on a) activities from the old organisation which need to be preserved, and b) any new ones needed to ensure the new organisation will deliver its new targets.

If the transformation is complex an attempt should be made to subdivide the organisation into discrete departmental or functional blocks which can be considered independently. For example if both old and new organisations have a sales organisation it may be possible to reorganise the sales department as part of a discrete transformation block. This is because sales staff in the new organisation will probably be sourced from experienced sales staff in the old organisation. Likewise the accounting department may be considered as a discrete transformation block. Although every transformation requires some degree of job flexibility it is generally unlikely that salesmen will be expected to become accountants and vice-versa.

After deciding which transformation blocks are appropriate a process is required to map the transformation of activities from the old to the new organisation within each block. This process can be structured using a trans4map. The trans4map lists the jobs of the old organisation (or transformation block) on the left. For each job the 'old' activities are listed. These are taken from the 'A' category in each job's value-TRAI. For each activity a simple metric is also included. This metric describes, for an average year, the percentage of a full time employee's time that is needed to complete the activity. For example, if an employee is expected to spend one fifth of his or her time on the activity the metric is 20%. This metric is called the 'employee-year %'.

If the employees in the old organisation were fully utilised these employee-year percentages for each job should add up to 100%. A traffic light colouring scheme is used to indicate the destiny of each of these activities in the new organisation. If the activity is coloured green it will be essential in the new organisation. If the activity is coloured red it is not

Chris Duggleby

required in the new organisation. Yellow activities are those which, whilst not essential, could be useful to the new organisation (sometimes referred to as the "nice to haves").

The essential 'old' activities listed on the left hand side of the trans4map are now allocated to jobs in the new organisation. These are listed on the right hand side. If a job is identical in both old and new organisations it can be excluded from this process.

The design of the new organisation starts by allocating all the green activities to jobs. The employee-year % metric can be used to ensure that the activities in each new job do not exceed 100% of a person's time. After allocating all the green activities, the yellow items can be allocated to appropriate jobs which still have spare capacity (in other words the job's employee-year % is less than 100%). The red activities will not move to the new organisation. Arrows can be drawn from jobs on the left to those on the right to demonstrate how the activities will flow during the transformation.

At the bottom left hand side of the trans4map is a box listing any activities required in the new organisation that did not exist in the old organisation. This box is called the 'in-TRAI'. These activities are also allocated to new jobs on the right hand side of the chart. Arrows can again be used to demonstrate the flow of new activities from the in-TRAI to their new jobs.

At the bottom right hand side of the trans4map is a box for any activities which were in the old organisation but are not required in the new one. This box is called the 'out-TRAI'. These activities are mainly red although some of the yellow ones may also be discarded into this box.

Arrows connect the activities leaving the jobs in the old organisation to go to the out-TRAI.

The diagram on the next page shows schematically the structure of the trans4map (for ease of presentation the Employee Year % numbers are omitted):

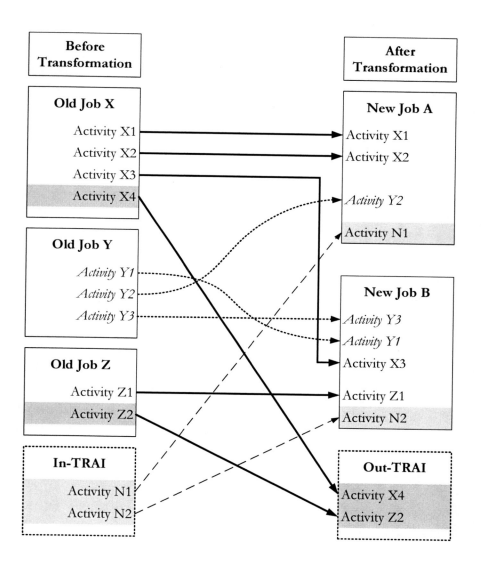

Figure 10: Job Change Trans4map

The job trans4map provides a framework to ensure that all of the essential activities from the old organisation are covered by new jobs. It also confirms how many new jobs will be needed to just cover these essential activities. This approach encourages discipline because it requires an early decision about exactly which activities are essential to the new organisation. It also identifies in one place (the out-TRAI) all the activities which will be taken out of the organisation.

Using the transformation block approach a job trans4map can be used for both simple and more complex reorganisations. In a complex organisation each transformation block (e.g. Sales, Procurement, Manufacturing, Accounting, etc.) will have its own trans4map.

Populating the in-TRAI

When preparing the trans4map essential new activities are placed into the in-TRAI. This in-TRAI can then be expanded to include the key targets, resources and interactions associated with each new activity. This important step helps to ensure that all the activities planned for the new organisation will have sufficient resources. It also encourages careful consideration of the key targets or objectives for these new activities before the change occurs. Identifying the required interactions will help to ensure new activities are aligned and coordinated with the other activities or entities in the organisation to facilitate a smooth integration and implementation.

Using the job t-TRAI with a trans4map

As mentioned earlier, the job t-TRAI is used to identify the elements of a job which change during a transition. It also identifies any transition specific targets, resources, activities and interactions. A job t-TRAI is used for every job in the new organisation where the activities have changed from the old organisation. Each t-TRAI can be created by using the following four steps:

Step one: Populate the job t-TRAI for each new job with changing activities.

The t-TRAIs for each new job are first populated with the activities which will undergo a change. This also includes activities which do not change but where the person doing the activity changes.

If an activity existed in the old organisation and is expected to be carried out in the same way, by the same person in the new organisation it does not need to be included in a job t-TRAI. In such situations where there is no change, risks to the activity are minimal. It is, however, important to ensure that the activities that do change refer to important interactions they have with these non-changing activities. These will be key to the management of risks to business continuity.

For example consider a transformation that does not require any changes to the sales team but involves the outsourcing of accounting activities to India. In this example sales people are expected to contact customers who are late paying their bills. Prior to the change they have received this information from the accounting department. Therefore the t-TRAIs for the accounting activities also need to refer to the interactions they have with the sales team. These are captured in the interactions section of the t-TRAI for the relevant credit control job in the outsourced accounting activity.

Step two: For each activity add the associated resources, interactions and targets to the job t-TRAI.

Once all the changing activities for each job t-TRAI are identified the changes to targets, resources and interactions associated with these activities are added.

The new targets, resources and interactions for each activity can be identified from the relevant old job value TRAI (where the activities existed before the transformation) or from the in-TRAI (for new activities). Sometimes an activity may exist in both old and new organisations but it may have a new target or different resources or interactions. For example the Sales-Accounting example described above involved a changing interaction. Often transformation projects require activities to be carried out in the new organisation using fewer resources (e.g. people or time) or at lower cost (and usually both).

One way to identify these value element changes is to consider how the activities in the old and new jobs differ in terms of their targets, resources and interactions. For each changing activity ask the question "How have the targets, resources or interactions changed?" For each new activity ask the question "What new targets, resources, and interactions will be needed to carry out this new activity?"

Step three: Identify transition specific (transient) targets, resources, activities and interactions for each job t-TRAI.

After a t-TRAI for each new job has been populated with the changing T, R, A, and I items the other important transition specific items must be considered. Although the same TRAI categories are used, here they are

Chris Duggleby

specific to the transition process: they will either be required to implement the change or be consumed by it.

The following simple questions can help to identify transition specific TRAI items:

- Does the transition process require resources, for example employee time or expenses?

- Does the new incumbent of this job require any special training in order to perform the new activities?

- Is the incumbent of this new job required to teach any other people how to perform their activities?

- Does the change require any change-specific communications? Usually such communications are required to support changing interactions; these could be internal interactions (other departments) or external ones (customers, suppliers, authorities etc).

- Does the change interact with any other business activity or process which could be disrupted or have its capability to create or protect value reduced (e.g. could the change impact business continuity)?

Step four: Add a timetable for all important changes to the job t-TRAI

Finally a time-table for each changing value element is added to the job's t-TRAI. This is particularly important when the change in one item depends on the prior completion of another item. For example training may need to be completed before a specific new activity can start. In addition resources (machines, raw materials, and the utilities needed for changed activities) may also need to be in place before a new activity can begin.

Usually the details and timing of individual changes to resources, activities (including communications activities) and interfaces are linked into a comprehensive project management programme. This is required to ensure all the various changes occur in the correct sequence, that resources are promptly available, and that communications are occurring at the right time. A holistic project management programme can also facilitate the identification of potential project efficiencies. For example, several people may require the same training or the communications and engagement activities for several job changes can be combined.

Using the job t-TRAI to manage risks

Once the job t-TRAI has been prepared it can be used like any other value TRAI to identify risks associated with the transformation. The main difference with using a job t-TRAI to structure a DOSER workshop is that the process starts by reviewing the changing job activities and then addresses their associated targets, resources and interactions (A standard DOSER workshop starts by reviewing targets). Each activity is taken in turn and the risks arising from changes to its targets, resources and interactions are identified. The criterion for identifying change risks is based on their potential to influence the value targets set for the transformation project or for the new organisation. Therefore risks are identified which could either influence the successful implementation of the project or influence the successful achievement of the goals identified for the new organisation.

Once the risks associated with changing activities are identified the DOSER workshop focuses on the transition specific targets, resources, activities and interactions listed at the bottom of the t-TRAI. Questions which can help this process include:

- Will the transitional facilities, like training rooms and equipment, be adequate?
- Will the job incumbents have sufficient time available during the transition to either receive training or teach others?
- Are communications about the transition clear?
- Are the communications aimed at the right people?
- Do the communications use the best media?
- Are there any risks to the continued operations of other business activities or processes (business continuity risks)?
- Are there any risks which will impact the timely delivery or budget of the transition targets, activities, resources and communications?

After completing the list of threats and opportunities for each job these can be used as a basis for a V&LIUMM evaluation and entered into the transformation project ExposureTracker. The output will be a risk management plan which includes actions and monitoring activities to deal with both the occurrence and consequences of important transition risks.

These actions and monitoring activities can then be linked to the transformation project management budget, plan and schedule to ensure a coordinated approach to managing the risks associated with the people involved in the transition.

Emptying the out-TRAI

During the creation of the trans4map all the activities which will not be required in the new organisation are placed into the out-TRAI. The out-TRAI can be used to monitor whether the benefits expected from the reduction in activities actually materialise.

In addition to listing activities the out-TRAI can provide a framework to capture the targets, resources and interactions associated with these 'departing' activities. Usually a transformation achieves savings by reducing the resources used by the organisation. Often resource savings are derived from the number of people which can be removed from the organisation. By adding up the employee-year % measures associated with the out-TRAI activities it is possible to calculate the number of full time jobs which will not be required in the new organisation.

As well as controlling the number of jobs which are removed from the organisation it is also possible to use the out-TRAI to check which other resource savings can be made. Normally when an activity is removed from an organisation there will be other savings like office space or other facilities (for example: company cars for sales people, computers for office staff). These resource items can be identified using the static value TRAIs for the old jobs from which the departing activities are derived.

By checking the targets associated with out-TRAI activities it is possible to identify whether an essential company target is being put at risk by, for example, the removal of a key activity which is needed for the target delivery. Likewise important interactions needed for the business can also be reviewed. Sometimes a departing activity has an interaction associated with it which may need to be reallocated to another job. For example a sales person covering a geographical area may also maintain an important relationship with machinery producers or other stakeholders in the same area. Removing the sales activity for that area may also put the relationship with these key stakeholders at risk. This interaction will therefore need to be reassigned to another job.

In addition to using the t-TRAI to help identify and manage important job change risks the out-TRAI can provide a basis for assessing whether the change project will actually achieve its delivery objectives.

XI. Process Risk: Static and Changing Processes

E valuating processes as risk subject can follow a similar approach to that already described in the previous chapter for jobs. Like jobs business processes can vary considerably in terms of size and complexity. Very complex processes can be broken down and simplified using a process hierarchy approach similar to that used to break down large business entities. These complex processes are divided into their component sub-processes which, if necessary, can be further subdivided into even simpler process elements.

In the last chapter the methodology for evaluating risks associated with jobs was described. Jobs were classified as either static or changing. In order to identify risks to static jobs they were defined using a static job value TRAI which was then used to structure a DOSER workshop. Risks identified in the workshop were evaluated using V&LIUMM and their management actions were controlled using an Exposure Tracker.

Most, if not all, of the static processes in a company will be part of somebody's job. In most cases this will be the job of the process leader.

Therefore when a company's risk management process is based on evaluating the risks associated with every job this should automatically include risks to processes since these will be part of the process leader's job description (which can be defined using the value TRAI for that job).

A separate, discrete, risk management approach for a process is only required if this brings additional focus to important risks associated with that process. Such a discrete, process based, focus may be worthwhile when the identification of process specific risks requires additional, specialist, expertise which was not available during the risk assessment for the process leader's job. In a DOSER workshop for a process the contribution from appropriate process experts plays a key role in ensuring the quality and quantity of the process risks identified.

In the previous chapter the process for jobs which were undergoing change was supplemented by the addition of two new tools; the job t-TRAI and the trans4map. These helped to ensure risks associated with the transition are effectively managed. The job t-TRAI was used to capture value elements (targets, resources, activities, interactions) which were related to the change. These were either: incremental to the old job's value TRAI (there were added to, or taken away, from it in creating the new job), or they were specific to the transition process and were therefore transient in nature.

An analogous approach can be used for processes. However, before this can start more complex processes may need to be broken down into simpler components. These simpler components are referred to as process elements. This simplification step is particularly important when managing risks associated with processes undergoing a significant change or which are part of a transformation project.

To break a process down into its process elements a simple process flow chart is required. Normally this process flow chart has the primary input to the process on one side of the chart. On the opposite side is the primary output. Although a process may have several inputs and outputs the conversion of the primary input into the primary output is normally the main purpose or "raison d'être" of the process.

For example, in a clothing manufacturing process, the primary input might be a textile garn like wool and the primary output might be a pullover. In a service example the primary input might be a request from a customer for information. The primary output would then the answer to the customer's request.

Some processes can be described as 'multipurpose': each purpose undertaken by the process may involve a different primary input or output. In the case of clothing manufacturing, the process may be capable of making different kinds of garments. This multipurpose variant may be able to select wool, cotton or acrylic garn as its primary raw material input depending on the purpose being undertaken. At the other end of this multipurpose process flow chart the choice of primary products may include: pullovers, cardigans or skirts.

As well as primary inputs, a process may also require secondary inputs or resources, some of which are consumed by the process, for example, electricity or lubricants. Other secondary inputs required by the process, will be fixed in nature, for example, machinery or buildings. Using the value TRAI terminology these secondary inputs are included under the resources category.

In order to convert a primary input into a primary output the process may involve several steps; these steps are used as the basis for defining each of the process elements. One way to simplify the identification of these process elements is to look for intermediate products on the way from the primary input (or inputs) to each primary output. Each of these intermediates will be the output of one process element and the input for the next.

For example, a production process to manufacture a chair may have as its first primary input a piece of wood. In the first process element this wood may be cut into smaller pieces. These pieces are "intermediates" which then become the inputs to the next process element where the pieces of wood are joined together. After joining the pieces of wood another intermediate "the unpainted chair" is created. This then becomes the input to the next process element in which the chair is painted. The painted chair is the next intermediate and becomes the input to the next process element where the painted chair is dried in an oven. After drying in the oven the completed chair is the final primary output from the process.

This example was based on a manufacturing process but the same approach can be applied to create a flow chart for a service process. Consider a service to deal with customer enquiries; here the primary input may be a phone call from the customer and the desired primary output is a satisfied customer. Process elements include: a) taking down details of the enquiry, b) deciding how to get the information needed to deal with the enquiry, c) connecting the customer with the most appropriate person to help them with their enquiry, and d) closing the enquiry by checking the customer is satisfied with the information received.

The key value creating characteristics of each process element are described using a value TRAI. Once the main targets, resources, activities and interactions are identified a process element value TRAI can be used as the basis for risk identification, evaluation, prioritisation and management using the standard tools which have already been described (DOSER workshop, V&LIUMM methodology and the ExposureTracker).

Static Process Evaluation

Processes which are not undergoing a significant change are referred to as static processes and can be evaluated in a similar way to static jobs. As explained above they can be either evaluated as part of the process leader's job or treated as a discrete risk subject focusing only on the process. Static processes convert primary inputs into primary outputs but the fundamental nature of the process is not undergoing a major change or transition.

These static processes are broken down into their process elements and a value TRAI is prepared for each. This value TRAI is used to structure a DOSER workshop and identify opportunities and threats. The risk evaluation then follows the standardised approach using V&LIUMM methodology and risk management actions are tracked using the ExposureTracker.

Let us consider how this works using a simple example involving a logistics department. CarNob Ltd's logistics department receives delivery orders (the primary input) from the sales department. These orders are processed through a number of steps until the correct consignment of CarNobs arrives at a domestic customer's factory (Primary Output). Each of these steps is a process element and the process flow chart can be visualised as shown in the diagram on the opposite page .

Each process element in the process flow chart performs an activity and has its own primary input and primary output. These, together with the targets and resources, are what characterise the process element. In the process element value TRAI, the resources include fixed resources: like equipment, and consumable or convertible resources: like energy or raw materials. In industrial processes the raw materials for a sub-process are sometimes referred to as "work in progress" (partially converted products from an earlier process element):

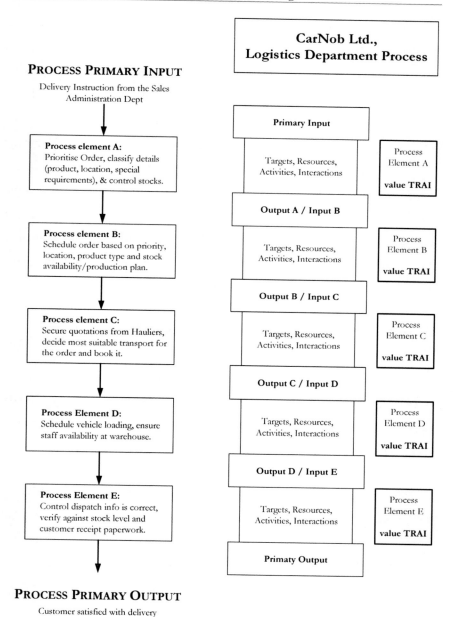

Figure 11: Dividing a Process into Process Elements for Risk Evaluation Purposes

Normally, in the preparation of a value TRAI the primary inputs to a process or process element are key value elements under the 'resources' category. They are among the most important resources for that part of the process. The primary outputs are included in the 'interfaces' group. This is to emphasize that the outputs are often not simply physical products or basic services. They actually fulfil some need or desire of: a customer, another department, or the next process element. Outputs do not simply satisfy a physical demand but are usually part of a performance package which can include: promptness of delivery, product quality, reliability and support service. These can all be significant interface exposure areas and this is why the primary output is dealt with as one of the key value elements in the interfaces category of the value TRAI.

Processes in Transition: The Process Trans4map

The approach described above explains how a process is broken down into process elements which can then be used as risk subjects in a risk evaluation. This is relatively straight forward when the process under review is static but what about processes which are undergoing change?

When a process undergoes a change the risks associated with the transition from the old to the new process must be managed. The old process is described using a static value TRAI. The new process also has a static value TRAI which describes the attributes of the process after the change has occurred. The changes in moving from the old to the new static value TRAI are described using a process t-TRAI. As with the job t-TRAI a process t-TRAI describes the incremental changes to the process targets, resources, activities and interactions and uses these same four categories to describe the transitional items needed for, or consumed by, the change.

This special adaptation of the value TRAI emphasises those items needed for the change which are transient in nature like training, teaching, communications and other project management related resources. This approach is illustrated in the next figure.

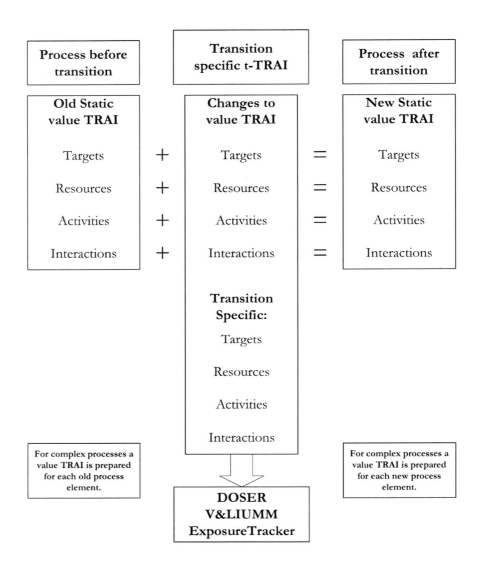

Figure 12: Identification & Management of Risks Associated with a Process Change

Using this approach complex processes are broken down into process elements using the process flow chart approach explained earlier in this chapter. In the flow chart each process element has its own value TRAI. When several process or process elements are being transformed with activities being combined, discarded or modified a process trans4map can be used. This is analogous to the trans4map described for job transformation projects in the previous chapter.

Let us consider how this works in practice. Prior to the process transformation a value TRAI is prepared for each process or process element that is likely to change during the transformation. The design of the new process is based on process activities (the A part of the value TRAI). Some activities will simply be transferred from the old to the new process, some will be new or changed activities which will be required to ensure delivery of the new process targets, and some activities will be discarded or outsourced.

The mapping of the transition of activities from the old to the new process uses the process trans4map. In this the old process elements are positioned on the left. For each process element the activities from the old value TRAI are listed. For each activity a simple metric is also included.

This metric is used to measure an important resource which is consumed by the process. If the key objective of the process change is to reduce the number of employees the metric 'employee years' can be selected. This measures the number of full time employees needed to operate that activity in one year. Other types of process changes may require an alternative choice of key objective. For example – if a reduction in machine time is the prime deliverable for the change 'machine-hour consumption' may be a more valid metric.

As with the previous application of the trans4map a traffic light system is used to indicate the destiny of each of the activities. If the activity is coloured green it will be essential in the new process. If the activity is coloured red it is not required by the new process. Yellow activities are those which whilst not essential could be useful (the "nice to have" activities).

The green activities listed under the 'old' process elements on the left of the trans4map are used to initiate the design of the new process. The new process elements will be described on the right hand side. All the green activities from the old process elements are identified in appropriate positions in the new process elements. Arrows are used to highlight the connection between old and new positions. Each activity includes the metric described above. The red activities will not move to the new process.

At the bottom left hand side of the process trans4map is a box listing those activities required by the new process which did not exist in the old process. This box is called the 'in-TRAI'. Arrows show the flow of these new activities from the in-TRAI to their position in the new process elements.

At the bottom right hand side of the trans4map is a box for any activities not required in the new process which existed in the old process. This box is called the out-TRAI. These activities are mainly red. It is possible that some of the amber activities will also be discarded into this box. Arrows connect the activities from the old process to the out-TRAI.

The diagram on the next page shows schematically the structure of the process trans4map (for ease of presentation the metric has been omitted). Clearly the design of the new process requires more than a collection of

Chris Duggleby

some old activities and a few new ones. Appropriate process design experts are required to ensure that the structure of the new process actually works. Together with the input from these process design experts, the process trans4map provides a Change Management Framework for capturing the important changing activities and the key items associated with them. These can then be used to structure a 'transition' risk identification and evaluation process.

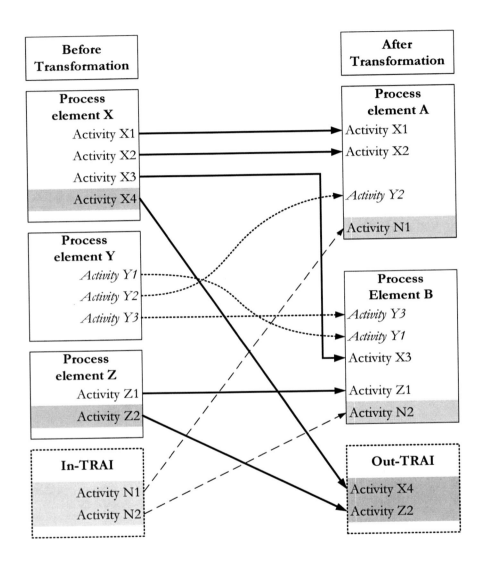

Figure 13: Process Change Trans4Map

The process trans4map documents the essential activities from the old process which will be included in the new process. It helps to track the prime deliverable for the process change through the use of the metric. It encourages discipline because its completion requires an early decision with relevant expert input about which activities are essential in the new process. The out-TRAI describes in one place all the activities and the amount of the key deliverable (via the metric) which will be taken out of the organisation. The in-TRAI formalises the decision about which additional resources will be required for the new process.

Populating the in-TRAI

When preparing the process trans4map any important new activities that will be required in the new process are placed into the in-TRAI. This in-TRAI can then be populated with the key targets, resources and interactions required to deliver these new activities. This step is important because it ensures the resources needed for the new activities are identified early in the transformation process. It also ensures that the targets or objectives for these new activities are carefully considered before the change. The interactions ensure that the new activities are aligned and coordinated with other process elements or other parts of the organisation. This helps to facilitate the smooth integration and implementation of the new process with the existing organisational structures and processes.

Using the process t-TRAI with a trans4map

The process t-TRAI identifies any changing value elements in moving from the old to the new process value TRAIs. It also identifies any purely transition specific targets, resources, activities and interactions. A process t-TRAI is required for every process element in the new organisation where the activities have changed from the old organisation. It includes special transition specific items, like training and communications, which support the preparation for and implementation of the process change.

The process trans4map was used to define the new process elements using the main activities required by the new process. A process t-TRAI should then be created for each new or changing process element. If an activity existed in the old process and will be carried out in the same way in the new process it does not need to be included in the process t-TRAI. In such situations where there is no change, the risks to these activities are minimal. It is however important to ensure that for activities which do change that their process t-TRAI includes their important interactions with these non-changing activities.

All the changing activities are placed into the process element t-TRAI. Once all the changing activities for each t-TRAI are identified the changes to targets, resources and interactions associated with these activities are also added.

Where activities exist before the change the targets, resources and interactions for these activities can be identified from the relevant old process value TRAI. For new activities the targets resources and interactions are identified from the in-TRAI. Special attention should be given to any important new targets or changed resources or interactions. By considering all the value TRAI elements it is possible to build up a comprehensive picture of all the process changes involved.

The identification of value element changes can be made easier by reviewing how old and new process activities differ in terms of their targets, resources and interactions. For changed activities consider how the targets, resources or interactions have changed: For new activities consider which new targets, resources, and interactions will be needed.

After the process t-TRAI for each new process element has been populated with the incremental T, R, A, and I items the other important transition specific items must be added. The same approach described above for job changes is followed. TRAI categories are used again but here they are specific to the transition: they are either required or consumed by it.

Typical questions to help identify these transition specific TRAI items include:

- Does the transition itself require resources, for example employee time or expenses?

- Do the people performing the new activities require any special training?

- Are the people who carried out the old process activities required to teach other people how to perform these activities?

- Does the change require any change-specific communications? This includes communications related to both internal interactions (e.g. other departments), or external ones (e.g. customers, suppliers, authorities etc)?

In addition to managing risks caused by activity changes the process change project will have its own project specific risks which need to be managed. The approach to managing such risks was described in chapter dealing with project risk.

Finally a time-table for each changing value element is added to the process t-TRAI. This is particularly important when the change in one item depends on the prior completion of another item. For example training may need to be completed before a specific new activity can start. Resources, like machines, raw materials, and the utilities needed for changed activities, will also have to be in place before the activity can change.

Typically descriptions of key changes to resources, activities and interactions and the schedule of their implementation should be linked into a comprehensive project management programme for the change. It is important to ensure that all the various changes are coordinated and monitored to ensure they occur in the correct sequence and that resources are available and communications are occurring at the right time. It will also help to identify potential additional project management efficiencies. For example, cost efficiencies may be possible by combining training, communications and engagement requirements for multiple activity changes.

Using the process t-TRAI to manage risks

Once the process t-TRAI has been prepared it can be used in the same way as any other value-TRAI. The difference with the process t-TRAI is that it focuses only on those process activities which are changing together with their associated targets, resources and interactions. It is used to provide the framework for a DOSER workshop which in this case is structured by addressing each changing activity in turn (rather than using the target based approach). For each activity the risks arising from changes to targets, resources and interactions associated with that activity are identified. The criterion for identifying risks is based on their potential to influence value associated with the key targets for the process change.

Chris Duggleby

Once the risks associated with changing activities are identified the DOSER focuses on the transition specific targets, resources, activities and interactions at the bottom of the t-TRAI. For example:

- Will the facilities, like training rooms and equipment, be adequate?

- Will the people involved in the changes have sufficient time available during the transition to either receive training or teach others?

- The following communications related questions should also be considered:
  - Are the messages clear?
  - Aimed at the right people?
  - Using the best media?

- What are the risks associated with delivering the transition targets, activities, resources and communications on-time?

- Are there any risks to the continued operations of other business activities or processes (business continuity risks)?

After identifying the threats and opportunities for each process element these can be used as the basis for a V&LIUMM evaluation and entered into the process change ExposureTracker. The output will be a risk management plan which includes actions and monitoring activities to deal with both the occurrence and consequences of important risks.

These risk management actions and monitoring activities can then be linked to the overall project management (budgeting, planning and scheduling) system to ensure a coordinated approach to controlling the risks associated with the process elements undergoing change.

Emptying the out TRAI

During the creation of the trans4map all the activities which are not required in the new process are placed into the out TRAI. The out TRAI is used to monitor whether the benefits expected from the change actually materialise.

In addition to listing activities, the out TRAI can be used to monitor which targets, resources and interactions are associated with the 'departing' activities. Usually a transformation achieves savings by reducing the resources used by the process. The main saving often relates to the number of people or another valuable resource which should, after the change, be used more efficiently by the process. By totalling those metrics identified with the out TRAI activities it is possible to predict the reduction in full time jobs or the other valuable resource once the new process has been established.

As well as monitoring the removed of these 'metrics' from the process it is also possible to use the out TRAI to check whether other efficiencies can be achieved. With each activity taken out of the process there may also be savings in workspace and facilities like equipment and systems. These resource items can be readily identified by comparing resources in the old and new process element value-TRAIs for the departing activities.

Checking the targets associated with departing activities in the out-TRAI may indicate whether essential company targets are being put at risk by, for example, the removal of a key activity needed to deliver them. Likewise key interactions needed for the business can also be reviewed. Sometimes a departing activity has an interaction associated with it which may need to be reallocated to another part of the process. For example another department may share part of a process which is being removed. This requirement needs to be addressed before eliminating that part of the process.

XII. Risk Management Communications

Communications can play a key role in helping to manage a risk's influence on business value. The 'I' category of the value TRAI describes the interactions a risk subject needs in order to deliver its targets and create or protect value. By supporting these interactions a well designed communications plan can be an important risk management tool.

Typical Stakeholders Influencing Target Delivery by a Risk Subject

During the preparation of a value TRAI, interactions were identified by first considering who the risk subject's key stakeholders were. The following is a generic list of typical stakeholders:

- Customers
- Suppliers
- Competitors
- Employees (Permanent and Temporary) and their Representatives

- Owners/Shareholders/Lenders/Auditors
- Governments (local, regional, national, international)
- Non-governmental authorities/rule makers
- Industrial bodies and creators of standards
- Interest/pressure/lobby groups
- General Public, representatives and influencers
- Other departments/functions

These interactions with key stakeholders are used as risk identification prompts in a DOSER workshop. The risks are prioritised and evaluated using V&LIUMM methodology and action plans are developed to minimise the damage from threats and maximise the benefits from opportunities. These action plans normally include some communications activities, particularly where risks are identified which relate to interactions.

Interactions generally flow in two directions; either the stakeholder needs or desires something from the risk subject or the risk subject needs or desires something from the stakeholder. For example, the stakeholder may require a product or service from the risk subject and in return the risk subject requires money from the stakeholder.

A risk management communications plan starts with a list of key stakeholders on the left-hand side. These stakeholders are identified from the risk management actions in the ExposureTracker. The generic list of stakeholders given in the table on the next two pages can be used as a check-list.

Next to the stakeholder list are two columns; one is for the needs that each risk subject requires from the stakeholder; the other is for the needs

Chris Duggleby

that the stakeholders require from the risk subject. To illustrate this, the generic list of typical stakeholders presented on the next pages identifies typical 'needs' in both directions.

Not all of these 17 stakeholders will be applicable to every risk subject; they are included in the list for illustration purposes. The value TRAI of a typical risk subject should have a maximum of 15 key interactions.

Very specialised risk subjects may have some very specific interactions which are not included in the selection given in this table. For example if the risk subject is a product development department it may also need interactions with universities, colleges and other technical experts.

Stakeholders	What the risk subject needs from them...	What they need from the risk subject...
1. Owners/ Shareholders	1. Continued investment, minimum day to day interference with how we manage the business	1. Profitability and increase in value of their investment. Security of their investment.
2. Providers of finance/debt	2. Continued investment at minimum cost, minimum day to day interference	2. We deliver what we promise. Security of investment
3. Higher management (above the risk subject)	3. Allocate finance to us for our investments and operations, minimum day to day interference	3. Our business and projects deliver what we promise and on schedule, no nasty surprises.
4. Project Leadership (within the risk subject)	4. Commitment, competence, lead by example, motivate the team	4. Interesting, correctly resourced projects with the potential to impress and get promoted
5. Employees inside the risk subject and their representatives	5. Competence, motivation, good team work and value for money	5. A competitively rewarded long term job working in a good team
6. The risk subject's 3rd party staff and service providers	6. Competence, value for money, availability, flexibility, minimum long term obligations and costs	6. Profitable opportunities to work or serve. Repeat work/ orders.
7. Other Leaders in the Company (outside the risk subject)	7. Provision of shared resources and special skills/experience.	7. Provision of shared resources and special skills/experience.
8. Other employees in the Company (outside the risk subject)	8. Good applicants for vacant positions in our risk subject, specialist help when needed	8. Career opportunities from the risk subject. Shared benefits from risk subject successes
9. Politicians (local, Regional, National)	9. Support to get permits, subsidies, tax breaks. Reputation and brand reinforcement	9. Taxes and to be associated with any success which will support their re-election.

Chris Duggleby

10. Law makers	10. Laws which support the business. Early warning of any issues (laws impacting business)	10. Legal and ethical compliance of our business. Specialist support when they draft new laws
11. Lobby Groups/ Non-governmental associations or pressure groups	11. Low profile unless activities of the group supports the business or influences other stakeholders	11. They want to draw attention and support for their interest areas and grow their influence
12. Industry Groups/Issuers of industry or technical standards	12. Early notification of changes which could influence business value. Opportunities to influence business relevant standards	12. Support. Involvement with the group's activities and its development of standards to give them credibility and influence
13. Law enforcers/Anti-cartel and Competition authorities	13. Confirmation that our activities are legal and protection from others who do not comply	13. Transparent, legally compliant activities and support for law enforcement activities/initiatives
14. Competitors	14. Fair competition. No attempts to involve us or other competitors in anticompetitive activities	14. Fair and legally compliant competition
15. Customers	15. We want them to buy from us in line with our marketing plan	15. A quality/price/performance product or service package which is better than the competition and makes their business successful
16. Suppliers	16. A quality/price/ performance product or service package which is better than other suppliers and makes our business successful	16. They want to sell to us in line with their marketing plan
17. General Public (local, regional, national)	17. A positive opinion regarding our business which supports our other communications objectives	17. They want reassurance that what we are doing will benefit them and their families.

Table 21: Risk Subject – Stakeholder 'Needs' Table

The needs identified in both directions are important inputs to the preparation of the communications plan. The next stage in this process involves the design of key messages for each stakeholder. These should be designed to support whatever it is the risk subject needs from the stakeholder. However, to be effective these messages must also take into consideration what the stakeholder needs or desires from the risk subject. The table on the next pages takes the generic list of stakeholders and, for illustration purposes, shows some typical communications messages.

Although the messages given in the table are very broad they demonstrate some of the key items which might need to be addressed for high level risk subjects, like a company or a major business division.

Every risk subject will have its own set of very specific interaction 'risks' and the messages should be tailored to address these risks. This process normally follows on from a risk evaluation of the risk subject using a DOSER workshop and a V&LIUMM analysis. These processes will feed a number of risk control actions into the ExposureTracker database. Normally several of these risk control actions will involve communications with stakeholders. Therefore the ExposureTracker action list is a key source of information for identifying stakeholders and messages to be used in the communications plan.

Stakeholders	Possible messages about the risk subject
1. Owners/Shareholders	1. There is a good fit between this business and the company strategy because it.............../The following valuable growth opportunities are being maximised by ..../The following important threats are being controlled and their impacts minimised through ....
2. Providers of finance/debt	2. The following items from our Profit/Loss & Balance Sheet confirm our track record for delivering on promises........./ This track record will be further improved by maximising the following opportunities and minimising the impact of the following threats ....
3. Higher management (above the risk subject)	3. Same as for owners/finance providers – but supported by more detail and tailored to the requirements of the individuals involved
4. Project Leadership (within the risk subject)	4. This Project is important to the strategy of the business because of.................. / The characteristics of the project and its risks need your special competencies and leadership skills to ensure success
5. Employees inside the risk subject and their representatives	5. This business is important to the company strategy because of.........../ Your role within the business is key to its success because of.............../ A good performance should open up the following opportunities for career development...............

6. The risk subject's 3rd party staff and service providers	6. In providing competitively priced services not available in-house you are a key contributor to this important business. Your adaptability and flexibility will help us continue identifying other opportunities for you.
7. Other Leaders in the Company (outside the risk subject)	7. This is a good business for the company which will benefit from your support and expertise. Likewise we will try to help your business.
8. Other employees in the Company (outside the risk subject)	8. This business has the following vacancies for capable/experienced candidates with a good track record of delivering good results........./ Volunteers for peer review groups are needed in the following........
9. Politicians (local, Regional, National)	9. This business helps to create/protect local jobs. It will enhance the local and regional economy (and tax revenue) and boost the national and local image as a profitable location for investment
10. Law makers	10. This business needs appropriate laws to create/protect employment and generates tax revenue. Please consider using our experience when drafting or changing laws which could impact our business.
11. Lobby Groups/ Non-governmental associations or pressure groups	11. The following information will help you to understand how our business supports the objectives of your group ....(if the groups objectives are totally at odds with the existence of your business avoidance of direct communications/contact may be appropriate)

12. Industry Groups/Issuers of industry or technical standards	12. The following information will help you to understand how our business supports the objectives of your group ..../ To support the development of standards for our industry we will make the following experts available.........
13. Law enforcers/Anti-cartel and Competition authorities	13. We welcome opportunities to work together and encourage full compliance with all laws. Let us know if there are any areas of concern and we will cooperate fully (during investigations be cooperative/open)
14. Competitors	14. Avoid non essential direct communications without prior legal advice. Openly discourage anticompetitive activities.
15. Customers	15. Our product/service package is better for you than the competition/alternatives because .... (include non-physical attributes in the package such as quality/reliability/support)
16. Suppliers	16. We are a good customer for your products because........... (emphasize 'non-price' benefits to the supplier – e.g. prompt payment history, advance ordering, any other relationships with the supplier)
17. General Public (local, regional, national)	17. This business makes a positive contribution to society by providing jobs, paying taxes and being environmentally responsible.

Table 22: Typical Key Messages for Stakeholders

After identifying the key messages for each stakeholder group, the most appropriate media to transmit these messages must be selected. Sometimes the same media channel may be used to deliver messages to a number of stakeholders. The table on the following page illustrates how the different forms of media and the stakeholders in a risk subject can be combined into a matrix to present a simple overview of the communications channel options.

Stakeholders	Private meeting	Presentation	Telephone call	E-mail	Our Internet site	Letter	Flyer/Leaflet	Local Press	Regional Press	National Press	Trade Press	Financial Press	Regional TV	National TV
1. Owners/Shareholders	X											X		
2. Providers of finance/debt	X	X												
3. Higher management	X		X											
4. Project Leadership	X													
5. Employees inside the risk subject and their representatives		X	X	X										
6. The risk subject's 3rd party staff and service providers	X			X										
7. Other Leaders in the Company (outside the risk subject)	X		X	X										
8. Other employees in the Company (outside the risk subject)			X	X										
9. Politicians (local, Regional, National)								X	X	X				
10. Law makers	X	X												
11. Lobby Groups/ Non-governmental associations or pressure groups	X	X												
12. Industry Groups/Issuers of industry or technical standards	X										X	X		
13. Law enforcers/Anti-cartel and Competition authorities	X							X	X	X				
14. Competitors		X									X			
15. Customers	X	X	X	X	X		X	X	X					
16. Suppliers	X	X	X	X	X			X	X					
17. General Public (local, regional, national)		X			X		X	X	X				X	

Table 23: Media/Stakeholder Matrix for Communications

Communications Accountability

Communications messages need to be delivered clearly and unambiguously through the most appropriate media channel to the correct recipient. There can be a number of reasons why a communications plan does not deliver the expected result:

1. The wrong stakeholder is being targeted
2. The needs of the stakeholder are misunderstood
3. The message is wrong
4. The message is being delivered through the wrong media
5. The person communicating the message is wrong
6. The timing of the message is wrong

The previous sections of this chapter addressed items 1) to 4). Much of the effort put into managing these four items can be wasted if there is not a clear system of accountability for communications delivery which all participants understand and comply with.

The delivery of each message, to each stakeholder, through the appropriate media channel is the responsibility of a Communications Accountable Person or CAP. The CAP performs a role which is discrete from that of the risk subject's Target Accountable Person (TAP) and their nominated Risk Accountable Person (RAP). For a very simple, low-level risk subject these three roles may be held by one person. For example, if the risk subject is a junior employee's job, that person could be responsible for delivering the job's targets, managing the risks to those targets and delivering any communications to support the management of the risks.

However, for more complex higher-level risk subjects a greater degree of specialisation and expertise is required in order to deliver these three discrete accountabilities effectively and efficiently. Consider, for example, where the risk subject is a division within a company which manufactures and sells components to car manufacturers. The Target Accountable Person or TAP for this division will be the manager of the division. This person would probably be too busy to manage all the risks to his business so he will delegate this to a number of Risk Accountable People or RAPs.

If this car component company is large it may have a Media Communications Office which is outside of the risk subject. Therefore the TAP may make the Media Communications Manager the CAP for all communications via Newspapers and TV. For risks related to customers the TAP may delegate the role of RAP to the Sales Manager since this is closely related to his job. Perhaps as part of his job the sales manager is also responsible for all direct customer communications (visits, letters, phone calls, e-mails). This means that for customers the Sales Manager is both the RAP (accountable for sales risks) and the CAP (specifically for sales related communications).

The Media/Stakeholder Matrix already described can be adapted to create a Media/Stakeholder Accountability Matrix. Here the CAPs are superimposed over the previous matrix using a simple Key. This means that if anybody needs to know who the accountable person is for communications through a specific channel, to a specific stakeholder group, they just need to refer to this table. An example of the completed Media/Stakeholder Accountability Matrix is given on the next page.

Stakeholders	Private meeting	Presentation	Telephone call	E-mail	Inter/tra-net site	Letter	Flyer/Leaflet	Local Press	Regional Press	National Press	Trade Press	Financial Press	Regional TV	National TV
1. Owners/Shareholders	A	A										B		
2. Providers of finance/debt	B	B										B		
3. Higher management	C	C	C	C										
4. Project Leadership	C													
5. Employees inside the risk subject and their representatives		D		D	D		D							
6. The risk subject's 3rd party staff and service providers	E			E		E								
7. Other Leaders in the Company (outside the risk subject)	C	C	C	C	C									
8. Other employees in the Company (outside the risk subject)				D	D									
9. Politicians (local, Regional, National)	F		F					G	G	G			G	G
10. Law makers	F		F							G				G
11. Lobby Groups/ Non-governmental associations or pressure groups	F	F								G				G
12. Industry Groups/Issuers of industry or technical standards	H	H								G	H			G
13. Law enforcers/Anti-cartel and Competition authorities	I													
14. Competitors		I									I	I		I
15. Customers	J	J	J	J	G	J	J	G	G	G	G	B	G	G
16. Suppliers	E	E	E	E	G	E	E	G	G	G	G	B	G	G
17. General Public (local, regional, national)		C		C	G		C	G	G	G	G	B	G	G

Table 24: Media/Stakeholder Matrix for Communications

Chris Duggleby

The letters on this Media/Stakeholder Communications Accountability Matrix refer to the following positions:

- **A**   Company Chief Executive
- **B**   Company Financial Executive
- **C**   Risk Subject's Target Accountable Person
       (its manager/leader)
- **D**   Risk Subject's HR Manager
- **E**   Risk Subject's Procurement/Contracting Manager
- **F**   Company Political Affairs Manager
- **G**   Company Press/TV Communications Manager
- **H**   Risk Subject's Technical Manager
- **I**   Company Legal Manager
- **J**   Risk Subject's Sales Manager

This definition of accountability is important. It can help to avoid duplication and confusion. The CAP finalises the communications plan for a specific risk by applying his or her experience and expertise to delivering the communications objective. This objective, including the proposed timing and high-level draft of the message are usually part of the risk management actions described in the ExposureTracker. The communications plan uses the most cost effective solution to ensure efficient message delivery. The CAP performs this task on behalf of the RAP and is therefore accountable to the RAP for the delivery of this part of the risk management action plan. Once the message has been delivered, the CAP reports this to the RAP together with any supporting information confirming the effectiveness of the communications activity in delivering the risk objective (e.g. Opinion Surveys, Media Feedback, Sales Trends etc.).

Here the CAP is acting as a service provider to the RAP. The RAP maintains overall accountability for managing the risk. He or she has been delegated this risk accountability by the TAP who maintains overall accountability for delivering the risk subject's targets. The Accountability flow is therefore:

TAP > RAP > CAP > Communication

Monitoring/Feedback > CAP > RAP > TAP

The communications design and control approach described in this chapter can be used to prepare a communications plan for any risks identified in an ExposureTracker. An example of such a risk specific 'CommsPlan' is given below. This example addresses the following risk:

Risk

Employees in a car component manufacturing company take industrial action (for example a strike) after they hear that some manufacturing operations will be moved to a low labour cost country.

The risk specific CommsPlan template is used to link the communications activities and the relevant media and stakeholders to the risks identified in the ExposureTracker. It also traces accountability for delivery from the Communications Accountable Person back to the Risk Accountable Person and finally back to the Person Accountable for the delivery of the risk subject targets.

The CAP > RAP > TAP accountability trail is an important part of risk management governance: a subject which has grown in importance following a number of high profile risk management failures in major corporations. The person responsible for delivering profits (the TAP) is also responsible for managing the risks to profit delivery. This person can delegate elements of the risk management to specialists (RAPs and CAPs) but still holds the ultimate accountability for managing risks to business profit.

Risk specific CommsPlan

Risk Subject	Car Component Production Division
Target Accountable Person	Division Director - **C** (see key used for Media/Stakeholder Matrix)

Risk Identified: Threat to normal production from industrial action when employees learn some production will be moved to lower cost, overseas, location.

Risk Accountable Person	Division HR Manager – **D**
Value TRAI Target(s) Influenced	Annual Production Target, Customer Satisfaction, Company Share Price (Reputation)
Main Stakeholder	**Production Employees**

Message: Transfer of low value production is essential to the future of this site as a base for making high tech products. It will increase the average profitability of remaining products made here making the site attractive for new high-tech investments. An estimated X job losses will be met by voluntary redundancy and early retirement.

Delivery Channels	Description of interaction	CAP	Date
Media #1	Meetings with Employee Representatives	C	DDMMYY
Media #2	Presentations to Employees in groups	D	DDMMYY
Media #3	Letters of explanation to each employee	D	DDMMYY
Media #4	Local Press Interviews/Advertisements	G	DDMMYY

Additional Stakeholder	**Local Community**

Message: The products being transferred abroad can not be produced profitably in this country. Job losses will be kept to a minimum and met by voluntary redundancy and early retirement. Moving low tech production out will allow this site to focus on profitable high-tech products and make it a more attractive for future investments. This will improve long-term prosperity and job security for the region.

Delivery Channels	Description of interaction	CAP	Date
Media #1	Meetings with local political leaders	C	DDMMYY
Media #2	Presentations to local communities	C	DDMMYY
Media #3	Local Press Interviews/Advertisements	G	DDMMYY
Media #4	Open Day after new high-tech equipment installed	C	DDMMYY

Table 25: Risk specific CommsPlan

Chris Duggleby

The wrong timing of communications can seriously reduce their effectiveness and in some cases actually work against the risk management objective. Consider for example the release of information to the press about an innovative new product development before sufficient stock has been manufactured to satisfy the surge in demand.

Communications scheduling is therefore an integral part of the CommsPlan for each risk. The actions described for each stakeholder and each media channel include a time for delivery. These are important risk management milestones which need to be planned, monitored and reviewed together with other risk control milestones described in the ExposureTracker. Planning for milestone achievement and risk management action delivery is particularly important in transformation projects. Here the transition specific t-TRAIs and the ExposureTracker produced from them feed information directly into the project planning process. Planning, monitoring and controlling delivery of risk management actions over time can be carried out using a Plan4mation chart. This is built up from information in the ExposureTracker and Communications Plans and is described in the next chapter.

XIII. Planning TRAI Information: Plan4mation Charts

Following the V&LIUMM risk evaluation process the key risk management actions were captured in the ExposureTracker and where necessary expanded using risk specific CommsPlans. Both tools include timetables to describe when actions or communications should be delivered. The Plan4mation chart is a tool which helps to manage the scheduling of these time based risk management actions.

A Plan4mation chart captures planning information associated with risk management and is structured using the four value TRAI categories which have been referred to throughout this book: targets, resources, activities and interactions (hence the reference to 4 in the name Plan4mation).

It can be used for planning risk management activities for single or multiple risk subjects. After evaluating a risk subject's risks using V&LIUMM the resulting management actions are logged in the ExposureTracker. The actions can be taken from the ExposureTracker and entered directly onto a Plan4mation chart using the four categories of the value TRAI classification.

A Plan4mation chart can be applied to both non-changing (static) risk subjects and to risk subjects undergoing a change. This means it can be used to plan the risk management activities for a person's normal static job or when the job is undergoing a significant transition. The latter situation often occurs in a business transformation project.

When multiple risk subjects are under evaluation the plan4mation chart can be structured using the same hierarchical framework as that used for the risk subjects. If this hierarchy follows the company's formal organisational structure the resources, activities and interactions at a given level in the organisation are a combination of the same items from lower in the organisation. Therefore resources scheduled in a higher level plan4mation chart are a combination of the resources required by all the lower level plan4mation charts from which it has been built up. This facilitates planning and monitoring at different levels in the organisation.

The table on the next page is a simple illustration of the general structure used in a Plan4mation chart. In this simplified example only one single small project is described which has a single deliverable target.

Chris Duggleby

Plan4mation Chart	Targets (deliverables & milestones)	Resources (physical, people & info)	Activities (incl. training & teaching)	Interactions (incl. Communications)
January		Before 31Jan Order alarm equipment RAP = E	Plan project RAP = C Design alarm system RAP = H	Get expert input to Project risks (DOSER) CAP = C Get expert input to risk mgmt action plan CAP = C
February	M'stone: 28Feb system delivered TAP=E		Train old operator on new system and prep. training for new operator RAP = D	Present plan for approval to Board of Directors CAP = C
March	M'stone: 31March recruit in place TAP=D	Recruit new operator RAP=D	Install new alarm system RAP = H	
April			Old operator teaches new recruit how to perform his job RAP = D	Intro. new recruit to system supplier CAP=E Intro new recruit to Police CAP=I
May		Training & info manuals RAP=H	Test new system RAP=H	Inform staff of new system CAP =D Inform Police of start date CAP=I
June	Delivery: operational alarm system TAP=C	Certified quality & safety of operating system RAP=H	Operate new system RAP = H Schedule future reviews of system quality RAP =H	Document learning's from project CAP=H

Table 26: Plan4mation chart for new security alarm system and recruitment of an additional operator

Planning Risk Management Information: Static Risk Subjects

When a risk subject is not undergoing a major transition it is described as 'static'. A 'static' risk evaluation process is relatively straightforward starting with a definition of the risk subject using its value TRAI. The Value Elements are then used to identify risks in a DOSER workshop. These risks are evaluated and management actions designed using the V&LIUMM process. Finally an ExposureTracker documents the control actions, together with the name of the Risk Accountable Person (RAP) and the timetable for delivery with appropriate milestones.

All of these items feed directly into the Plan4mation chart. Each risk management action will each have its own simple value TRAI. Its targets, milestones, resources (including people and information), activities and interactions can be entered into the appropriate columns on the chart. As described in the previous chapter when risks are associated with interactions these may require a CommsPlan. The details from the CommsPlan (stakeholder, message, media, timing and Communications Accountable Person) are entered into the interactions column of the Plan4mation chart.

Normally only material risks are included in the detailed risk control process. Since it is used to plan and schedule all the material risk control actions, a comprehensive Plan4mation chart will be much more detailed than the illustrative, simple, example above. Therefore at the very least a computer spreadsheet programme is recommended for Plan4mation chart preparation. This can then be formatted and subdivided to suit the specific requirements of each risk subject.

Chris Duggleby

If several risk subjects are to be included these can be allocated their own "pages" in the spreadsheet. This approach can be particularly useful with a risk subject hierarchy because a higher-level chart can be designed to provide totals from the resource or communications requirements described in the lower charts. This works very much like an accounting programme in which the contents of cells in departmental spreadsheets (e.g. containing costs) are collated and totalled in the divisional level spreadsheet.

Planning Risk Management Information: Risk Subjects in Transition

The t-TRAI has been introduced to capture value TRAI elements specifically associated with risk subjects in transition. The t-TRAI is used to structure a DOSER workshop to identify transition risks and then V&LIUMM is used to evaluate these risks and design risk management actions. This is analogous to the process described above for static risk subjects. Therefore the ExposureTracker used to capture the information from a risk subject in transition can be used in the way already described to feed a plan4mation chart.

The only difference with a risk subject in transition is that the risks identified relate to resources, activities and interactions specifically associated with the transition. Once the transition is complete the plan4mation chart should no longer be required. It is therefore described as a transient plan4mation chart.

XIV. Getting more help

This book is part of a broader initiative to help businesses introduce more efficient and effective risk management processes. It is the first step in documenting and communicating a number of simple tools which have been designed to help companies introduce and implement risk management systems. These tools have not been created in some remote seat of academic learning but are derived from first-hand experience in one of the most dangerous industries in the world.

I am fortunate in having spent over 30 years managing chemicals businesses and their associated risks across the world with a number of internationally respected partners. As a result of this hands-on experience I have developed a strong reputation as an implementation focused risk manager. Most recently I have been involved in the design of Management of Change processes and in assessments of risk management and compliance programmes for major global businesses.

The tools described here have been designed with implementation in mind. If you think something does not fit perfectly in your organisation try out those elements that appear to work well and consider adapting the other tools as appropriate. This book reflects the current stage in the evolution of these processes and they will certainly evolve further as the value TRAI approach receives more interest and improvements based on constructive feedback can be developed.

I have had to restrain myself in this first publication. There are many processes and tools presented here which could probably justify a book in their own right. With time I hope to rectify this and I am already involved in developing other modes of communication, including an e-based Risk Tuition website (under the name 'RiskTuition.com').

To promote fast and easy access to information about risk management processes and tools I have opened an internet portal at www.bizchangers.com. This will give basic information about some of the tools described here and also provide access to the RiskTuition system. As software systems are developed to facilitate the organisation of risk management processes these will be made available via the bizchangers.com portal.

One of the most important things I have learned from many years working around the world is that feedback is an essential part of process improvement. Peer reviews and seeking expert advice have been recommended on a number of occasions in this book (the DOSER workshops). My objective to continuously improve business risk management capability is very much dependent on how well this book is understood and implemented. I will therefore appreciate hearing from you if you have any constructive feedback or suggestions. I can be contacted directly via the e-mail link at www.chrisduggleby.com.

XV. Table of Figures

XVI. Table of Tables

Lightning Source UK Ltd.
Milton Keynes UK
20 March 2011

169603UK00001B/1/P